D0820281

I WANT
TO TAKE YOU
HIGHER

I WANT TO TAKE YOU HIGHER

THE LIFE AND TIMES OF
SLY & THE FAMILY STONE

JEFF KALISS

Backbeat
Books

An Imprint of Hal Leonard Corporation

New York

Published in 2008 by Backbeat Books
An Imprint of Hal Leonard Corporation
7777 West Bluemound Road
Milwaukee, WI 53213

Trade Book Division Editorial Offices
19 West 21st Street, New York, NY 10010

All lyric excerpts from "If You Want Me to Stay"; "Fun"; "Everyday People"; "Stand!"; "Don't Call Me Nigger, Whitey"; and "Jane Is a Groupee" published by Warner-Tamerlane Publishing Corp. and Mijac Music. Used by permission.

Printed in the United States of America.

Book design by Publishers' Design and Production Services, Inc.

Library of Congress Cataloging-in-Publication Data is available upon request.

ISBN 978-0-87930-934-3

www.backbeatbooks.com

Contents

Contents

Foreword

BOY, THE YEARS GO BY FAST now. I've been looking at it like, between this Friday and the next Friday, it seems like it's getting shorter and shorter. I'm using my time right, but it's always that pursuit of happiness. There's more happiness, but the one you're looking for, I think, stays the same distance away.

This world is different, but it's the same difference with another name. If I didn't play music from now on, I wouldn't be a musician—and I'm gonna hang in there whatever happens. I'm still doing music, and still representative of the truth. I like playing with everybody, but I can only harmonize with a few. If everybody from the old band could afford to get together and stay together for about a month and then go to play gigs, that would be cool. We do love to play with each other.

I don't read much of what anybody writes about me, but I know that it's mostly secondhand stuff that looks like it's supposed to be firsthand. I don't know nobody, and nobody knows me, and they don't know what they're talking about. But I see why they say some things that they consider negative, especially when it has to do with what will sell their damned things.

I like the way Jeff tells my story. It seems level, and it seems on the level. He keeps how I look at things separate from anybody else's looking at things. I'm only craving fewer pieces of paper, fewer words in my letters and fewer letters in my words, in order to say what I gotta say. The rest of it, like this book, happens natural, and everything's good after that. My opinion about things is still the same, and I'm pretty aggressive about making sure people hear it. They accept it easy, or they gotta accept it hard.

Thank you, Jeff.

—SYLVESTER STEWART/SLY STONE
From inside his '58 Packard
Napa County, California
February 2008

Preface

DAVID KAPRALIK CAME TO SEE my group at the Sugar Shack in Boston and he was blown away. He was ready to sign us as soon as possible.

I was overwhelmed. This was the dude—at the time he was a well-known Columbia Records executive.

Three weeks later, I walked into his office in New York and he was frantically rushing around. He laid some pictures out on the floor, on the table, all over the place, while giving me advice on our show—he talked about me being the center of attention, about being brighter and wearing brighter clothing, etc. He was comparing me to the guy in the pictures.

I had heard this comparison before—it was Sly & the Family Stone.

He said, "I better be right, because I am betting my life on this. I am my leaving my job here at Epic to manage him." At the same time, he was pulling out records and putting them on the turntable for me to hear, and he said, "Remember, it's different."

I said, "You're damn right it's different!" They were a mixed, beautiful group. Black, white, and big Afros. They looked like

Funkadelic on Motown! We were very similar, but dark. They looked like a polished version of us.

When the first record played, I didn't know what to think. Were they a white group? They had a strange pop sound. Their pop songs, like "Stand" and "Everyday People," were as pop as you could possibly get, but the black songs was as black and funky as Ray Charles and James Brown. They had the biggest Afros in the world. I thought it was a Bay Area thing, like Huey Newton.

"Sing a Simple Motherfucking Song" was *the bomb*! This was it. This song hit me just like "What'd I Say" by Ray Charles. It was the funkiest thing I had ever heard in my life, from Motown to James Brown to the Beatles. I knew then David knew what the fuck he was talking about. They were the complete package: they could play, sing, write, and produce, and all superior to anybody I'd ever seen or heard before. David had to pull me away—I was so into Sly's records that I forgot I had gone up there to sign a deal for myself.

David told me I would see for myself that night—he was taking me with him to see Sly.

The show was going to be at the Electric Circus, a small club in the East Village in New York. As showtime approached, I realized David had his hands full dealing with tickets, backstage passes, people, so I told him I would be okay, I would just get a seat.

I walked down to the West Side to a store called Paul Sergeant and got me some funky haberdashery for the night. I knew I had to represent. So many people had compared us.

I showed up at the Electric Circus by myself. I got some acid and I was so high, everything was beautiful, which was not unusual for the East Village on a tab of sunshine. When I arrived at the front door, they saw the look on my face and let me right in. This was a special night. It seems like everyone was high and happy.

It was a psychedelic club, with black lights, posters, side rooms with couches and dens. Everyone was sitting down, relaxing. All of a sudden there was a big commotion. People had been waiting for a good while, and all of a sudden all hell broke loose—I had never heard bass like this before, and one of our bass players, Billy Bass Nelson, would have eight cabinets, so I knew what bass sounded like! Larry Graham was loud as hell! They had the clarity of Motown but the volume of Jimi Hendrix or the Who. They literally turned this motherfucker out. That would be the impression that Sly left on me for the rest of my life.

"Jane Is a Groupee," "Plastic Jim," "Underdog," "Don't Call Me Nigger, Whitey"—whether political, social, or party songs, you always thought they were speaking directly to you personally. Not unlike Bob Dylan or Smokey Robinson.

David introduced me to Sly and told me that Sly had a new record label called Stone Flower, and would we like to be the first group on the label? Sly gave me a look, the one that I would recognize in time to mean he knew something was cool.

We signed with Stone Flower Records. The label folded after they put out just one record, by Sly's sister, but we stayed in touch. It would be years before I would see him again.

He came and spent a year with me on my farm, and we had a great time, writing songs and everything else. I inducted him into the Rock 'n' Roll Hall of Fame. I only saw him for a few minutes then, and then it would be years and years before I saw him again, to team up with him on my album *George Clinton and Some Gang-*

sters of Love. I don't know what it is about our chemistry, but we are always cool with each other. At the very beginning of the Mothership tours, he played four shows with us. Other than myself, he was the only person ever to come out of that spaceship!

—GEORGE CLINTON

Introduction

WOODSTOCK AND THE music that led him there four decades ago are still alive for Sly Stone. "There could be a Woodstock on this very hill, out there," he suggests, gesturing toward the sun-kissed acres of his rented property in Napa County, up the road a piece from his childhood home in Vallejo, California. "That's what I'm working up to now, again, something like that," Sly continues, in reference to his perennial late-night sessions in his private studio, eking out new tunes and lyrics for a public still caught up in the hits from long ago. Of course, it will never be "like that" again, and it doesn't need to be. Too much has changed for Sly, for the Family Stone band in which he played at Woodstock, and for the fans they shared that world with.

The spirit that had floated over the half million hippies sprawled across Max Yasgur's pastureland in the wee hours of August 17, 1969, was made from those times, redolent with marijuana, psychedelics, youthful hormones, and an adrenaline pulse of protest against the old, the tired, and the just plain wrong. The groups booked throughout the weekend of the Woodstock Music and Arts Fair had already helped set the accompaniment for the late sixties and the coming early seventies. The motley but consistently exciting and often rebellious acts included Creedence Clearwater Revival, Jimi Hendrix, the Jefferson Airplane, and Carlos Santana. But Sly & the Family Stone stood out against the happy haze. They not only played to the times, but they actually looked like the ideals held dear by their fans: black and white, male and female stood side by side on the stage, arrayed in fantastic fashions and hairdos, rallying the crowd to get "higher." All their songs, in fact, were rhythmic and uplifting, bass and drums providing an irresistible foundation for the flights of horns, guitar, and keyboards, and for the catchy vocals of sexy sister Rose and her sibling Sly—part shaman, part preacher, part trickster, part soul brother. His lyrics raised messages that might serve as musical picket signs: up with love, down with racism, turn on, free your mind!

To seek out the story of this man and this band, we need to look beyond the brief, bright glow of Woodstock. We go back to Sly's beginnings, as Sylvester Stewart, in gospel music, and through the Family Stone's start as a rhythm-and-blues cover band in San Francisco. And we continue past Woodstock on to a confusing time with darker messages, influenced by drugs and the other indulgences of celebrity, by the dissolution of the band, and by Sly's subsequent struggle to keep his gifts and his person from being extinguished by his loneliness and bad judgment.

There's much mystery and apparent contradiction in this story, not all of which can be resolved within any literary discourse on it. Sly is a black man, whose scrutiny by and punishment under the law may have been prejudiced by his race. Yet he rarely testified to his ethnicity or to contemporary civil rights struggles. Sly formed one of rock 'n' roll's most vital and visible ensembles, and partnered them in a set of high-energy performances and in hits that continue to live in movie soundtracks and commercials. Yet Sly was party to the premature end of that ensemble, and opted instead for a solitary, synthesized sound and a succession of pickup groups.

And now, after decades in which Sly & the Family Stone's legacy helped fertilize the blossoming of rock, jazz, funk, rhythm and blues, and urban musical styles, the mystery persists. The sexagenarian Sly has outlived some of those rockers who shared and succumbed to the same bad habits, among them Jimi Hendrix and Janis Joplin, as well as those like Marvin Gaye and John Lennon, who were victims of violence. But Sly has been slow to deploy the Family Stone in the sort of successful comeback enjoyed by such other veterans as the Eagles, Led Zeppelin, and the Police. Sly's own appearances with several Family Stone spin-offs have usually fallen short of the standard set by the original band. Yet he keeps making music and maintaining, "It'll all come together, and there will be a lot of help."

This suggests the story is still playing out. Old hits and old crimes must be examined for what they suggest about the people directly responsible and about the times in which they occurred. But this book is also about relationships, a sort of extended "Family Affair," and about how the good and bad vibes of some of these relationships continue into the present alongside the music.

My own first contact with Sly & the Family Stone came over the radio during my first months covering topics like civil rights and antiwar protests as a student journalist at San Francisco State, in the year of Woodstock. I loved every one of their new, surprising singles that made it onto the airwaves over the next few years: "Dance to the Music," "Stand!," "Sing a Simple Song," "Everyday

People," "Thank You (Falettinme Be Mice Elf Agin)," "Family Affair," "If You Want Me to Stay," and so forth. Soon after the last big hit, like many fans, I lost track of the man and the band. So it was exciting and easy, many years later, to accept the assignment to put the story of Sly & the Family Stone in print.

Making it happen was a slower, tougher process. Although there were feature pieces and reviews in periodicals from the band's heyday, there had been little since, and no biography per se aside from Joel Selvin's *Oral History*, a compendium of quotes published in 1998. I went through this material with a skeptical eye for bias, recognizing that there was little to be found in the way of substantial interviews with Sly himself. I did interview those few persons intimately involved with the story who were still alive and willing to talk about it, and I eventually got to Sly.

What emerged from all this was a portrait of a passionate talent—unpredictable, uncontrollable, and fantastic—which had been based in family, community, and friendship, and then extended into the wider world. The world was entertained, and arguably bettered, by its embrace of Sly & the Family Stone. The portrait also reflected on the peculiar and often perverse interdependence of media and celebrity, and on the pervasive influence that both have on the culture at large, which is all of us. Fame and fortune seemed to ultimately aggravate Sly's compromise of his personal integrity and of the integrity of his group.

I came to realize that the faith of Sly's blood family and friends, and that of his musical Family, had survived the decades of estrangement and resentment. Despite old bummers, these people seemed eager to see themselves now as part of a more positive and forward-looking legacy, more about making memorable music, both then and now. Looking back on Sly's story, however large and distorted the images may have become, we all can find familiar facets of our own humanity, hopes, challenges, mistakes, and achievements. *I wish I could*, Sly had sung in "If You Want Me to Stay," *get the message over to you now.* In Sly's many messages, and throughout this book, there are glitters of introspection and wisdom, as well as the makings of a great soundtrack.

—JEFF KALISS

Note on Style

T O REFLECT THE FRIENDLY and informal spirit of a family and a band, first names are used throughout the book after the initial use, or re-establishing uses, of each full name. Generally, the present tense is used with quotes from this author's interviews, and the past tense with quotes originating elsewhere, in order to distinguish the sources and to help forestall misunderstandings. The only exceptions to this usage comes in the stand-alone descriptions, in the past tense, of the author's two in-person interviews with Sly, and in the scene of Sly's return performance in 2007, where the author is clearly identified and the present tense would have proven awkward.

I WANT
TO TAKE YOU
HIGHER

Get Your Livin' Down

— 1943-1961 —

You live your life religiously, and you live your
life with mankind, trying to make sure that you
can deal with this world while you're here.

—JAMES BROWN
1993 interview with Jeff Kaliss

THE STEWART FAMILY OF Vallejo, California, had a reputation for making music, both in their own house and in several houses of the Lord. The earliest recording of Sylvester Stewart, later known as Sly, was a seven-inch 45-rpm disc with "On the Battlefield of the Lord" on one side and "Walking in Jesus' Name" on the other. It was recorded in 1952, on the recommendation of a local church official, when Sylvester was nine. He sang lead vocals alongside brother Freddie and sisters Loretta and Rose, and it was in the family, and their church, that Sylvester found his earliest musical and spiritual inspiration.

The family made occasional road trips to Denton, in northern Texas, to stay with relatives, perform in area churches, and peddle their recordings. Those travels brought the kids' mother, Alpha, back to her own roots as a daughter of the Haynes family, founders of the very musical St. Andrew Church of God in Christ, in Denton. The role of music in the sect, the largest Pentecostal group in America, seems related to what is described in Church of God documents as "supernatural manifestations," having occurred in Christ's time on the day of Pentecost, fifty days after Passover. "The sudden appearance of the Holy Ghost appealed first to the ear," the Church maintains today on its Web site. "The disciples heard a 'sound' from heaven which rushed with a mighty force into the house and filled it, even as a storm rushes, but there was no wind." No doubt the mind of young Sylvester and his siblings also received this apocalyptic spirit.

The history of Denton, Texas, Sylvester Stewart's birthplace, encapsulates an important portion of the history of African descendants in the United States, and the influences under which Sly and his family would be raised. Denton County's 1850 census listed five slave owners and ten slaves. These persons likely originated in Tennessee, Kentucky, and the Carolinas, and whites and blacks worked the fields side by side to subsist on the clay-based soil of the newly created state of Texas, which joined the Confederacy in 1861, four years after the founding of the city of Denton. Following the Emancipation Proclamation and the end of the Civil War, many of the former slaves evolved from servants to tenant farmers, and the development of cotton, wheat, and other cash crops expanded the influx of both races. The Chisholm Trail, regaled in a jaunty cowboy ballad, brought cattle from the South through Denton, and two major rail lines followed suit.

The settlement of Freedmen Town, in the area where Sly would be born seventy years later, was populated in 1875 by twenty-seven black families from Dallas. What would become an even larger and more active black community, Quakertown (possibly named for

Quaker abolitionists) took form a few years later, closer to the city center. Outside of farming and service jobs within Quakertown, the North Texas Normal College and the Girls Industrial College both became significant employers of blacks after opening in Denton (to white students only) around the turn of the century. Other Quakertown folk worked as daytime domestic servants of wealthy whites along Oak Street several blocks to the west. Pride of place in a growing Quakertown community ultimately fell victim to resentful white racists, who appropriated the area to establish a downtown park and fairground, forcing the black residents out of the downtown and into an area of failed former pastureland to the southeast. Many blacks opted to leave Texas, but those who remained strived to restore Quakertown's hard-won level of self-sufficiency.

In the meantime, blacks returned to being dependent on white services downtown. "We knew where we were supposed to go and we went where we were supposed to go, and we didn't go where we weren't supposed to go," recalls Betty Kimble of her life as a black teenager attending school with Sly's older cousins (including future college halfback and pro football Hall of Famer Abner Haynes) in 1940s Denton. "We'd sit in the back of buses, and go to colored water fountains, and at the restaurants we went through the back door."

As southeast Denton laid in retail outlets and services along Prairie Street, one of its two blacktop thoroughfares, the churches did their best to sustain hope and community spirit. The newcomer St. Andrew Church of God in Christ and its pastor, F. L. Haynes, must have seemed like novelties alongside the established Methodist and Baptist sects, which dated back to Quakertown. Haynes's congregation was "more free with their rejoicing and all," says Ruby Cole, who went to church and school with several of the pastor's offspring, Sly's cousins. Others remember that before St. Andrew was constructed, worship occurred outdoors under a tent, and intimidated passersby would throw things at the "hollering" parishioners. Eventually St. Andrew earned more respect for its music. The pastor's younger sisters, Alpha (Sly's mother) and Omega, led hymns with pretty, powerful voices. Alpha's husband, K. C. Stewart, who'd relocated to Denton from Fort Worth, fashioned a percussion instrument from a washboard, tin cans, and baking pans. This unique form of accompaniment joined in with the church's piano and numerous tambourines.

Into this joyful noise were born K. C. and Alpha's daughter Loretta in 1934, and son Sylvester on March 15, 1943, the first two of five children, all of whom would be raised in music. (Freddie Stewart would also inherit from his uncle F. L. Haynes a pastoral calling within the Church of God in Christ.) The growing Stewart family occupied a large white house on bustling Prairie Street. K. C. reportedly frequented the cotton and tomato fields, turning his percussion array to the purpose of entertaining and soliciting donations from the field workers. His wife, Alpha, worked as a maid in white neighborhoods, at least up until the birth of Loretta.

Not long after Sylvester's arrival, the family followed the path of several of Alpha's relatives out west to the San Francisco Bay Area, to seek a better life in an economy that had been stimulated by wartime industry.

Well-liked and dependable, K. C. Stewart found a home in Vallejo, a smaller city on the northeast outskirts of the Bay. The size of the black population in Vallejo increased dramatically during the '40s, jumping from 438 in 1940 to 1,513 in 1950, an increase of 345 percent. With modest income from maintenance work for a local department store and from other jobs, K. C. was able, with Alpha, to expand their family to Rose (1945), Frederick

(1947), and Vaetta (1950). In the San Francisco Bay Area, the children were able to envision possibilities far beyond those their parents had been limited to in Texas. *Black Stars* magazine, in 1972, relayed an anecdote from Alpha, in which her sons had been asked what they wanted to be when they grew up. "Freddie said he wanted to be a lawyer," she remembered. "Sylvester said he wanted to be a bishop." (To this day, Sly has plenty to do with lawyers, but it was his younger brother who himself became an ordained church official.) Back in the '40s and '50s, each of the Stewart kids in turn, and ultimately in ensemble, came to share their parents' celebration of music and of the church.

There was a strong musical presence in the local black churches, as there had been back in Texas, and Vallejo spawned at least one successful recording gospel group, the Spartonaires. As in Denton, there was musical migration between sects, and the Stewart kids sang all over the Bay Area. In *Mojo* magazine, mama Alpha later singled out young Sylvester, then nicknamed "Syl," as the star of these devotional routines. "They'd stand this bitty five-year-old on a table and he'd sing 'You Got to Move,'" she related. "People were hollering and wanting to touch him. You had to hold them back sometimes." For Syl's part, he was already sensitive to audience reaction, as recounted by his sister Rose in the 2000 Showtime documentary *The Skin I'm In*. "When we were little kids," she said, "if people didn't stand and applaud and really feel the spirit of what he was singing, he'd cry afterwards. It affected him that bad." A local church official urged the Stewart Family Four, formed from the eldest of the children, to further spread their appealing juvenile spirit in a 45-rpm gospel single. Syl, nine at the time of the recording, had picked up on his older sister Loretta's familiarity with piano. Mama Alpha, who played guitar in church, also introduced Syl to her instrument.

It could be supposed that potential musical influences, as with other opportunities, were more varied and eclectic for the Stewart children in the Bay Area than if they'd been raised in Texas. Young Sylvester might have developed as more of a bluesman and less as a forward-thinking re-imaginer of rock, though he did end up bringing to the mix some of the elements of blues and gospel that he shared with less influential Texans like Bobby "Blue" Bland and Junior Walker.

Across the city of Vallejo, the heritage of racism stayed in place, as it did in much of postwar America, but the lines were not as broadly drawn as in Texas. Each of the low-income neighborhoods in the Terrace section of the city, collections of plywood structures erected during World War II on the north side of Vallejo, favored a particular racial grouping, but the groups all lived in close proximity to each other. The Stewarts occupied a more prominent home on Denio Street on the western side, near the cemetery and the Mare Island Naval Shipyard, which had been a major source of income for blacks and others who flocked to the West Coast from elsewhere. Though there was some persistent de facto segregation among elementary schools in the '50s, it started to fade throughout the public school system. In junior high schools and in the three-year Vallejo High, and over Bay Area radio stations and television, young people of all colors experienced the irresistible evolution of rhythm and blues into rock 'n' roll.

Rock was a revolution that shook up stereotypes. White teenagers everywhere heard and watched white rock idol Elvis Presley crooning and shaking his hips in imitation of what he and his peers, including Jerry Lee Lewis and Conway Twitty, had observed, sometimes covertly, at Southern black churches and dance halls. Black teens, meanwhile, found their race represented alongside whites in the pantheon of early rock by such performers as Little Richard, Chuck Berry, and any number of black doo-wop groups. Rock may not yet have sought the sophistication of jazz (where black and white musicians were already relatively well integrated), but it had gotten beyond the narrow and restricted status of "race" music. Anyone could play rock 'n' roll, and everyone could listen to it.

Frank Arellano, the musically inclined son of a Filipino father (a welder at Mare Island) and a white mother, had upgraded from the Terraces to a middle-class east side neighborhood. He remembers meeting one of his future singing partners, Sylvester Stewart, newly nicknamed "Sly," when Sly came to play guitar behind a doo-wop vocal group at a dance. Both Frank and Sly were still in junior high. "Everybody in the singing group was waiting for him to get there," laughs Frank. "Does that sound familiar?" (Delays have indeed dogged Sly Stone performances, right up to his latest ones.) After Sly's arrival, Frank noted that the guitar was almost as big as its player, who was several years younger than most of the other members of the group.

Just before their first year of high school, Frank encountered Sly again during a summer league game of basketball. "It was an elbow here, an elbow there, and 'I'm gonna get you after the game.' So, after the game, everybody was outside and lining up. . . . Their team was all black, ours was mostly white. . . . I saw this skinny little guy, and I went, 'I'm gonna get across from him, 'cause he couldn't hurt me.' And that was Sly. We kind of squared off, a few things were said, and then everybody said, 'This isn't cool,' so nothing ever happened. Little did I know how fast he could be, so it was probably a good thing we didn't have that fight." At Vallejo High, though they were at the same grade level, Frank didn't share many courses with Sly. "Maybe he was smarter than me," Frank allows, "but I had a bunch of easy courses. I caught my high school counselor groping one of the young lady aides when I went in his office one time, and after that I got all the easy courses I could get, any time I wanted." It was Frank's musical inclination that brought him back in contact with Sly.

In junior high, with an all-Filipino group, Frank had sung doo-wop, a term coined in the '50s for the smooth, listener-friendly mode of vocalizing rhythm and blues, or R & B (itself named earlier in the decade by Atlantic Records producer Jerry Wexler). Frank had encountered another precocious doo-wopper, blonde Charlene Imhoff, at musical events and at baseball games, where she served as what he called an "athletic supporter," a suggestive way of tagging a loyal fan.

At Vallejo High, Frank and Charlene assembled several versions of a group they named for her junior high ensemble, the Viscounts. Sly at this time was singing and playing guitar with a black group, the Webs, who the Viscounts encountered at interscholastic talent shows. Frank told Charlene, "Our harmonies suck, and I'm gonna ask this guy I know if he'll come help us put some harmony together." That's how Sylvester Stewart came, somewhat reluctantly, to be recruited into the Viscounts, who happened, without deliberate intent, to be multiracial.

Aside from Charlene, Frank, and Sly, the Viscounts ultimately included brothers Charles and Vern Gebhardt, who lived a couple of doors down from Charlene, and Maria Boldway, a classically trained soprano and an alluring, raven-haired ethnic mix of Spanish, Mexican, French, and Native American. For performances, the girls lined up in flared dresses and high heels, the boys in blazers, slacks, and dress shirts, cinched by narrow ties. Their hair was as trim and maintained as their outfits.

After the group had begun to show professional promise, they were advised to change their name. There already was a group called the Viscounts, which had made a successful cover of the moody "Harlem Nocturne" in 1959, the year the Vallejo Viscounts' formed. The teens considered being called the Biscaynes, after a popular full-size Chevy model introduced in 1958, but ended up as the Viscaynes by substituting a *V* for the *B* to signal their hometown and to avoid confusion.

Despite the pressures of school and of most of the guys' athletic involvement (Sly avoided organized sports), the Viscaynes accelerated practice sessions to five evenings a week in the Gebhardts' rec room. They all had fine and flexible voices, with Sly able to sing high or low across a two-and-a-half-octave range, and Frank ascending in a heady falsetto. By 1961, when most of the group was in the last year of high school (Vern and Maria were two years younger), they felt ready to sing in a contest promoted by the *Dick Stewart Dance Party* television show, a San Franciscan echo of Dick Clark's nationally broadcast *American Bandstand*. They beat out the competition, appeared on local TV, and were placed under management by associates of the television host. As graduation approached, they were encouraged to record several 45-rpm singles, with dubbed accompaniment by Joe Piazza and the Continentals (including future Family Stone member Jerry Martini), at San Francisco's Geary Theatre. Less than satisfied with this effort, their new management flew them down to Los Angeles for another recording session (using songs written by husband-and-wife team George Motola and Ricky Page) and an appearance at a dance party event at Pacific Oceanside Park, alongside a young Lou Rawls.

Boarding at a hotel and recording and performing in Tinsel Town amounted to quite an adventure for the Vallejo adolescents. "We swam, we were treated like royalty," recalls Maria, commonly called "Ria" by her friends. "The boys ran around doing crazy stuff, dumping ice water on us when we'd be sleeping by the pool." Treatment by their handlers turned out to be chillier. In a move sadly common on the lower rungs of the music business, the Viscaynes were told to sign their checks for performing over to management, and they never got to bank any of the proceeds themselves. The Viscaynes' "Yellow Moon" placed at number 16 on KYA radio's Top 60 chart in the week of November 13, 1961, and stayed aloft for a few weeks, but the group had long since dispersed.

Inside and outside the Viscaynes, Frank Arellano had gotten closer to Sly than most of his schoolmates. "We were everyday friends," says Frank, now retired with his own teenage son in Palm Springs, California. "We would drink, do crazy things. We were always on the edge of the law, but never getting caught, never anything we could go to jail for." This reputation would have helped justify the morphing of "Sylvester Stewart" into "Sly." "And we were out trying to get girls," Frank continues. "We cruised downtown, mostly in Sly's car. He had a '56 Ford Victoria." When they had enough pocket money, the pair would extend their cruising west, across the Bay Bridge to San Francisco, where they could get girls to join them on the Ferris wheel at the Playland at the Beach amusement park. For this and other purposes, the underage party animals had to figure out how to find booze. Sly had copped an identification card from someone of legal age and had talked Frank into making use of it at a Vallejo convenience store, even though the cardholder's "race" was designated "colored." When Frank somehow succeeded in scoring a large green bottle of Rainier Ale, the friends shared a good laugh along with the intoxicant. Sly seemed to regard most racial issues lightly. Charlene recalls a Viscaynes gathering in the living room of the Stewart household and Sly entering the room from mama Alpha's kitchen.

"Now I know," he declared to his fellow Viscaynes sardonically, "how funny I must look in your house."

But in one rare instance, Sly shared with Frank a deeper reflection on being a young black man in the '60s, closer to what he'd express lyrically later in "Underdog," on the first Family Stone album. "He felt," says Frank, "that he was on a ladder, and that he was trying to climb up the ladder. And there were people above, pushing him down, and there were people below him, grabbing his legs and pulling him down. And that was his struggle, more or less. It is tough being black, I guess. But I'm glad he realized there were people of his own race trying to pull him down, and people of other races pushing him down. I never had that much of a problem."

There were problems, Frank also remembers, with interracial dating, even though Sly's natural-born attractiveness transcended any color barrier. Frank compares the young Sly with their black piano-and-trumpet-playing schoolmate John Turk, who'd known Sly since childhood and would continue their musical relationship into the 1970s. "The difference was, John Turk was kind of like a lounge lizard, everybody knew what he was there for, and John Turk was there just to go get some white women. Sly, on the other hand, was there and had white women go for him. . . . They bugged him, they'd call him, and I was there for some of those calls, the finest girls. He'd make a date with 'em, and then he couldn't go pick 'em up. So guess who did? Yours truly!"

Thus Frank found himself yet again pressed, or persuaded, into service for his buddy. "I'd say, 'How the hell do you think they're gonna like a Filipino pickin' 'em up any more than a black guy?' He goes, 'But, man, you're not a nigger.' It worked. We never had any problem. I got a few weird looks, but nobody told the girls, 'You can't go out with him.' Then the parents would say, 'But you guys be home by twelve.'" Frank would take the date to a pre-arranged meeting point, deliver her to Sly, and then connect with one of his own. "I'd say, 'Okay, be back here by 11:30 and I'll take her home.' But I'd have to wait till 1:30 or 2:00, and then take 'em home! Thanks a lot, Sly."

Frank thought that Sly shared everything with him, but he didn't realize how well his friend was living up to his new nickname. During the L.A. stay, for example, Sly had been taking side trips with songwriters Motola and Page to record solo projects without the knowledge of his fellow travelers. Back in Vallejo, Sly had started making recordings with his younger brother, Freddie, and others, and on some weekends sustaining his instrumental chops with club bands in the black part of the Terraces, also without telling the other Viscaynes that he might have competing gigs.

On a double date shortly before spring graduation in '61 (Sly had to wait and make up a unit in summer school before getting his diploma), Frank came to the realization that his best friend had been secretly carrying on a relationship with a sister Viscayne, Ria Boldway. More than any other member of the group, Ria seems to have been sensitive to racial issues in their community. She and Sly and John Turk all joined a group called the Youth Problems Committee, specifically to address these matters. Ria was also more interested than most of her white girlfriends, even as a preteen, in the rhythm and blues being beamed toward the Bay Area black demographic over KDIA radio. Ria now recalls how she'd been inspired by "Ray Charles and [jazz vocalist] Betty Carter performing together. And it's so funny, because even Sammy Davis was too square for me by the time I was sixteen. He wasn't funky enough for me."

Although she was two grades behind Sly, Ria shared choir practice with him, and apparently a certain amount of classroom mischief. Despite their superior voices, they both ended up flunking one semester of choir, having amused themselves by baiting a substitute teacher. As far as Ria knew, Sly got "great grades" otherwise, and was generally a standout among the student body. "He was a star before he ever became a star," she says. "He just glittered when he walked, like Richard Cory," in the poem by Edward Arlington Robinson, which was also a popular folk song.

Ria points to other juvenile harbingers of later Sly Stone behavior, including "his smile, and his ability to put everybody on. And I understood what he was doing, and most people didn't. He always told me I was probably the lamest person he ever knew, but, man, when people would talk to him or ask him things, he'd go off and say the craziest stuff, and I knew he'd be putting them on. And they'd just say, 'Oh, thank you, Sylvester!' "

Through all this, Sly began to count on Ria as a good friend in frisky female form. She'd follow him downtown on Saturdays, where daddy K. C. Stewart worked in the Higgins Building, and the friends would ride the elevator, one of the few then in town, for hours. It was during the formation of the future Viscaynes that Ria was shanghaied by Frank and Sly, who'd separately become aware of her musical training and ability. "I was walking across the campus one lunch hour," she says, "and they grabbed my arms on either side and said, 'You're coming with us.' And they took me over to Sly's mother's house. It was a nice home on a kind of hill, it wasn't in an extremely dangerous or bad part of town, and they had me sing for 'em. And Mama cooked us lunch, and that's when I became a member [of the budding group]."

After about a year, the friendly simmer between Ria and Sly heated up to a romance. "I wouldn't call it 'dating,' because that wasn't allowed [between blacks and whites]. I would call it"—she hesitates—"what would you say? I hate to use the word 'sneaking,' 'cause that's such a terrible word. But I don't know how many people knew. We tried to keep it under cover, because my father told Sly that he would kill him if he found out we were seeing each other. My mother is a very devout Catholic woman, and she only wanted my safety and [Sly's] safety, especially from my father or anyone else who would cause us problems because of it." In a few years, Sly would be ready and eager to hang out with white women in the open, though society wouldn't be ready to condone such relationships for a while longer.

Sly and Ria's romance built on their friendship. "We could tell each other secrets, you know, kid secrets," she says. "Talk about our dreams, spend hours on the phone together. Get away together whenever we could." In the meantime, they openly dated others with whom they wouldn't be violating any unwritten code. "I was dating the football captain," says Ria, "and [Sly] was dating a darling, tiny little black girl. I don't know how he felt about me going out with other people, 'cause I didn't 'share myself' with other boys. And I don't know whether he did, with this girl or any of the other girls I heard he'd seen." She did find out, by asking, that he'd bought his girlfriend a bedroom heater for Christmas, and she pronounced this act "kind."

On the Dick Stewart–inspired junket to Los Angeles, Ria found a legitimate reason to hang on openly and tightly to Sly: it was his first plane trip, and he was scared. She didn't know it at the time, but the hotel on Hollywood Boulevard that put the Viscaynes up was one of the few in the area to accept racially mixed groups at that time. After a late night of relatively tame teen fun, "I was the only one that would venture to wake Sly up," Ria points out. "No one else would dare, 'cause he would wake up swinging. I don't know what that was all about. But I would go into his room and just sit on the edge of his bed and sing to him. He'd go, 'I'm asleep!' and I'd go, 'No, no, it's time!' And he'd just get up, sweet as pie."

The bond between Ria and Sly held after his graduation, and hers two years later. The Viscaynes, though, didn't continue long enough to follow up after hitting the KYA charts in the fall of '61. Frank threatened to leave the group after the L.A. experience had revealed that he was in effect working for nothing, for shady management. The management then threatened to sue his parents for breach of contract, and Frank joined the Air Force, where he expected to escape persecution. Charlie went off to a university, while his younger brother, Vern, and Vern's classmate Ria, finished high school. Charlene got a job and got married. Sly, though, had already sensed that his fate lay in music, and he was determined to stay on course.

You Have You to Complete

— 1961-1966 —

Do you know what the secret of success is?
Be yourself and have some fun.

—Tito Puente

S LY STAYED AROUND VALLEJO and expanded his interests and skills with a variety of keyboard and stringed instruments, and harmonica, working them in a number of R & B bands. Shortly after graduating from Vallejo High in 1961, he also decided to focus on continuing his academic education, studying music theory with David Froehlich at Vallejo Junior College. David and Sly developed the sort of student-mentor relationship on which so much great achievement has been built, throughout the histories of both Western and Indian classical music, folk traditions, and more recently in jazz and pop. With uncharacteristic magnanimity, Sly has credited David for this again and again, on the liner notes to his albums, in his rare print interviews, and in TV appearances. And although they've spent practically no time together since those college days in Vallejo, the affection seems certifiably mutual, still treasured by David in his

Vallejo home, where he now stays up to speed on jazz piano and ready for the occasional gig, long past his retirement from the educational system.

David grew up south of Vallejo, in Oakland, in the 1930s and '40s, when he'd pay thirty-five cents to see and hear and maybe later chat with Count Basie, Duke Ellington, Jimmy Lunceford, Fats Waller, and other black jazz greats visiting Oakland's Sweet's Ballroom. After becoming a skilled pianist and being discharged from service in World War II, David entered a junior college in San Bernadino on the G.I. Bill and met his own mentor, a theory teacher named Russell Baldwin. "He was so deeply sincere about the value of music," David remembers about Baldwin, "and about how fortunate we were to be into such a field, which I've always believed since." Baldwin inspired his student to proceed to graduate study at the Eastman School of Music in Rochester, New York, from which David returned to the Bay Area, which in the '50s, looked and sounded quite hospitable to both jazz players and fans. Clubs abounded in San Francisco's North Beach, Fillmore, and Tenderloin districts. To help pay for his pleasures, David found stable daytime employment teaching music theory and English to a multiracial mix of high school graduates in Vallejo and leading their college dance band. "They were beaten, some could hardly read," he reflects, "but we had fun together."

In the early 1960s, David was approached by an intense young man he'd seen around campus, playing guitar at student assemblies. Sly Stewart told the teacher that he "wanted to do more, to become a professional. And he was in the position I was in when I started school in San Bernadino, never having heard the nine symphonies of Beethoven." For David, the classics of the Western canon were treasures he was eager to share, because "the longer we live, the more we realize their greatness, their truth, their majesty." The teacher made the old masters work for his pupils. "A big part of our program was ear training, based on the Bach root movement," says David. "The theory part was [from composer and academic] Walter Piston, but ear training was something different." David disseminated miniature classical scores so that students could see the structure of what they were listening to and noted that "Sly wasn't used to seeing such a thing." Years later, former Epic Records exec Steve Paley reports that Sly could be seen strolling through a studio with one or another of the Walter Piston theory tomes under his arm, a tangible influence on his distinct and sophisticated approach to popular music. For Sly, more so than for most rockers, informed sophistication mattered as much as unschooled instinct.

While he was still one among a roomful of music students, Sly's teacher noted that his star pupil "stood out, of course, as being intelligent and personable but with a complete anxiety to learn. He was not acquainted, had not had a chance, with the physics of music, acoustics, the overtone series, which the chord progressions of Bach are based on. All of this was new to this gentleman, and it fascinated him. When it came to such things as style and form and history, it's what he wanted to know."

As a role model for David and Sly, "Bach was an excellent ear man," the teacher points out. The eighteenth-century composer "could walk into a cathedral and say, 'The sound will come over that beam and across the ceiling, and be heard over there.' That was all new to Sly." However, Sly would display similar perception and attention to detail in his later work, orchestrating, arranging, and recording in the studio.

Sly's love of learning had him raising his hand repeatedly in class and remaining with more questions after other students had been dismissed. He shuffled attentively through not only Western classics but also his teacher's strongest suit, jazz. "We laughed about the song [famed jazz bassist] Ray Brown wrote, 'The Gravy Waltz,' " David recalls merrily. "When we got to the bridge, neither he nor I could remember it. He came back in the next day or two and said, 'I got the bridge!' and he hummed it out. That was something he did for me. When I think back, he wasn't listening as much as he was rehearsing, playing, and writing [in his mind's ear]."

Both David and Sly probably would have been very happy to prolong their mutual learning experience. But the day came when Sly had to leave academia for other adventures. "I didn't want to say much, I was listening," recalls the teacher about Sly's actual day of departure. "And he said, 'Don't worry, I'll be back to see you, in a limousine full of girls.' And [several years later], he was!"

IT WAS A FORTUITOUS TIME and place for Sly to be launching a career in popular music. He and the baby boomers, just a few years his junior, were listening to the radio, buying what they heard there, and going out to dance to the music, which in 1961 included Ben E. King's wistful "Stand by Me" and "Spanish Harlem," Ray Charles's imperative "Hit the Road Jack," Sam Cooke's smoothly polished "Cupid," and such melodramatic marvels as "Running Scared" by Roy Orbison and "Runaway" by Del Shannon. That was also the year Chubby Checker launched non-contact but sinuous dancing to "The Twist." Meanwhile, Berry Gordy had founded his prolific Motown label, and former Georgia cotton picker and shoe-shine boy James Brown, who'd been gigging and recording since the mid-1950s, began to earn a lucrative reputation as "the hardest working man in show business."

Sly could hardly wait to join this scene where blacks were hardly a minority. KYA-AM was among the most popular San Francisco rock stations in the early '60s. It had also proven a benign refuge for disc jockeys and close friends Tom "Big Daddy" Donahue and Bob Mitchell, who'd reportedly fled west from Pittsburgh's WIBG under threat of federal prosecution for the not uncommon practice of taking payola (basing radio playlists on bribes from record companies). "They had the East Coast radio technique down," comments Alec Palao, a rock archivist who has produced compilations of Sly's pre-Family recordings. "Donahue in particular had an incredible presence on the radio. He had this deep voice and this commanding manner," issuing from a jumbo-size body, "and he was talking the argot of the time, he had a lot of phrases. He [and Mitchell] took over KYA, and once they got that going, they really sent the ratings up. . . . They became very powerful as guys that would spot a hit and play it to death, 'breaking' it. That's how KYA got a reputation as a 'break' station [open to regional surprises and sudden crazes]."

The spontaneous sound of radio in that era, long before corporate depersonalization squelched that sound, was intoxicating to free spirits like Sly. He was thrilled when Tom Donahue and Bob Mitchell heard the potential in the Viscaynes' "Yellow Moon" and afforded the single some time on their drive-time playlists.

TV was also learning how to rock out as Bay Area baby boomers of all races flocked to the tapings of *Dick Stewart Dance Party*. Prominent in Stewart's early '60s telecasts, alongside future *Playboy* Playmate (and future Mrs. Dick Stewart) Barbara Burrus, was another hiply attractive and likeable youth with great dance moves, Sylvester Stewart (obviously no relation to the show's host), who also appeared on *Dance Party* with the Viscaynes. Sly also frequented live rock shows at San Francisco's Cow Palace, hosted by radio jocks Donahue and Mitchell under the aegis of Tempo Productions.

It may have been at one of these shows that Sly made the fateful acquaintance of the jocks/impresarios. In any case, the DJs, following their ambitions beyond arena shows and the airwaves, founded a label, Autumn Records, in 1964, and with remarkable foresight hired the much younger but equally ambitious Sly, who'd already impressed them as the de facto producer for the Viscaynes. In Autumn's studio, notes Alec Palao, "He'd be leading the band on the floor, jumping around, changing the arrangement, directing people. The role of the producer back then wasn't as defined." And Sly knew his way around a variety of instruments and musical styles. The studio served as a hands-on laboratory for the twenty-one-year-old Sly to apply his collegiate training in orchestration, to learn the mechanics of taping, microphone placement, and overdubbing, and to absorb the more subtle craft of songwriting while turning out a marketable product.

Within a year of signing with Autumn, Sly had proved his worth by creating the label's biggest hit record. Bobby Freeman had been one of the first San Francisco rockers (after ballad crooner Johnny Mathis) to place on the charts, with the playful, Latinized "Do You Wanna Dance," in 1958. There were lesser follow-up hits, but his "C'mon and Swim," in 1964, qualified as a dance craze. Bobby has credited Sly as the "composer, producer, and conductor" of the single and associated album. It happened this way: the veteran singer had been signed by Tom Donahue and Bob Mitchell to join in their Cow Palace shows, where Sly was providing production and instrumental duties and eventually leading the house band, in addition to his job in the recording studio. After one show, Sly engaged Bobby about his onstage movements, likening them to a swimmer's. Performer and producer then brought their brainstorm back to the studio, forging a gold record that climbed to the number 5 spot on *Billboard*'s pop and R & B charts, revived Bobby Freeman's career, secured Autumn Records' reputation, and started to bolster the name and bank account of the multitalented Sly.

"He arranged 'C'mon and Swim' with exciting breakdowns," comments Alec Palao, in reference to the song's periods of dance-inducing percussion, a technique later applied pervasively to disco and hip-hop. "Maybe to our ears they sound kind of clichéd, but [Sly] turned what could have been a pedestrian record into a very exciting record. He's on top of the groove, and that's a crucial thing in any form of music." Alec also attributes the Swim's success to "a little bit of serendipity: the sudden explosion of focus on . . . North Beach and that whole topless thing, which was a very newsworthy thing at the time." The band for "Swim" was basically Joe Piazza and the Continentals, with whom Sly had played bass in North Beach venues and who'd earlier backed the Viscaynes. The group, including future Family Stone saxophonist Jerry Martini, mutated into the Condors, backing popular featured act George & Teddy at North Beach's Condor Club, where Sly himself also appeared with a group called the Mojo Men.

The Condor began attracting lurid national attention when cocktail waitress Carol Doda initiated the practice of mounting the piano, removing her top, and dancing during band breaks. Doda later took over ownership of the Condor, and the former music hall was refitted as a flagship of North Beach's tourist-tempting strip club scene. This reputed revival of San Francisco's Barbary Coast reputation helped the Swim move onto dance floors everywhere, alongside the tamer Twist and Mashed Potato, and arguably helped establish alluring go-go dancers, topless or not, as a fixture at many major clubs. The fad flourished in San Francisco until then-mayor Dianne Feinstein prompted raids and bans in the 1980s. Today the Condor, tamer but still in operation, boasts state landmark status.

With some of the first big money that "C'mon and Swim" brought him, Sly helped his father move the Stewart family from their modest location on the outskirts of the Bay Area to a home in San Francisco's Ingleside district. Earlier in the century, the Ingleside, several miles southwest of North Beach and the downtown, was one of several areas where developers had established written and unwritten "covenants," in effect bylaws enforcing the image of a genteel white middle-class lifestyle that would exclude nonwhite residents. As recently as 1958, a cross had been burned on the front lawn of black judge Cecil Poole's house, who'd managed to buy a home in the Ingleside directly from its previous owner, rather than through realtors, who wouldn't have helped him. Poole accounted for the charred cross to his daughter Patti with the comment, "Some Christian has lost his way." The Pooles stayed put, and over the next decade, the Ingleside became a neighborhood of choice for middle-class black professionals.

The Stewarts' spacious homestead was located a few blocks south of the Pooles', on the ovular Urbano Drive, which had been a popular racetrack before the great earthquake of 1906. Sly moved along his own multiple career tracks in high spirits, sometimes speeding between appointments in a Jaguar XKE custom-painted purple, a reward from Tom Donahue. He appropriated the basement of his parents' house into a base of operations. He continued to perform, as did brother Freddie, in several bands, and to produce singles for Autumn, as well as waxing several of his own. Some of this material has been compiled by Alec Palao for Ace Records (based in his native England) as *Precious Stone: In the*

Studio with Sly Stone 1963–1965, released in 1994. The disc is the best showcase yet, outside of the Family Stone, of Sly's skill as a producer and of his understanding and application in songwriting of '60s R & B. Included are early rock collaborations with siblings Freddie and Rose, and with his then-new friend and keyboard mentor Billy Preston.

It was rare in the early '60s, and evidence of the greater opportunities available in the Bay Area, that a young black man was given access not only to professional studios (San Francisco's Coast and Golden Gate studios) but also to working with different kinds of artists. Sly was assigned several white rock groups, early representatives of what would come later to be embraced by the hippies as the "San Francisco Sound." The city's music scene was evolving, alongside the evolution of its counterculture, from Jack Kerouac and the Beats in the '50s to the starry-eyed flower children of the next decade. The new generation seemed to want to experiment beyond the influence of the Beatles-led "British Invasion." But most musicians weren't as experienced or as confident as Sly. Charged with devising make-or-break singles with musicians whose technical range might not allow for much formal sophistication, Sly learned to shape their talents into basic but very effective hooks, licks, and choruses.

Some white rockers, most famously the Beau Brummels, were in tune with their young black producer. The *Precious Stone* liner notes by Alec quote a couple of women who'd sung for Sly at the Coast studios, back when they were teens in Catholic school. "Here was this very flashy black man, dressed in Beatle suits and this weird pompadour," said Catherine Kerr. "He was strange! But he was always very sweet to us, always very protective. You know, 'Make sure you call your mom!' " Her schoolmate Melinda Balaam added, "Sly was always smiling. I've never been around someone who was so 'up' all the time." In those times, it still would have been a pretty natural high.

With other rock acts, like the Great Society and the Warlocks (antecedents of the Jefferson Airplane and the Grateful Dead, respectively) and the Charlatans, there was friction and sometimes open hostility. "They had their own ideas, but they didn't have the chops to back them up," says Alec about such groups. "As far as [Sly] was concerned, they were amateurs, and as far as they were concerned, he was Mr. Plastic-Hey-Baby-Soul. But at the same time, a lot of rock groups benefited from Sly being in the booth, because of his enthusiasm," not to mention the erudition the producer had absorbed from his teacher David Froelich. "That's why, when you listen to some of the Beau Brummels' session tapes [rough cuts], and you hear [Sly], you know he's focusing on getting them to sing right, have a great performance," Alec points out, "even though the group already had the goods and a style."

In the case of the Great Society, Sly reportedly put the group and its lead singer, Grace Slick, through two hundred takes of "Somebody to Love" and attempted to position himself on lead guitar. Grace ended up taking the song on to another group—the Jefferson Airplane—and to legendary rock status a few years later. The Beau Brummels, though, stayed with Autumn and scored the label's next (and last) national big hits, "Just a Little" and "Laugh, Laugh," both produced by Sly, with a deceptive sound evocative of the Beatles even though the Brummels were strictly Bay Area.

Sly's Autumn output was, in Alec's opinion, "more vanilla than you'd expect." It's revealing to listen to the Brummels' delivery of Sly's "Underdog" from their debut disc. It's reminiscent of the Rolling Stones' "Get Off of My Cloud" and far more upbeat than the Family Stone's version of the tune several years later. Like the racial makeup of the stellar band he'd later form, Sly created music in different colors, favoring elements from the white side of rock when it pleased him (and clients like the Brummels), but equally ready to deploy R & B (as he did on the Family's "Underdog"), and to meld the two influences with jaunty syncopation, at odds with standard R & B rhythmic patterns. Sly's youthful and multifaceted talent is also in evidence on his own recorded performances for Autumn. His "Scat Swim," one of several follow-ups to Bobby Freeman's big hit, didn't go very far, but it revealed a jazzy, scatting style of the vocalist perhaps unfamiliar to later fans and probably encouraged by David Froelich. Within the tracks of Alec's Autumn compilation, you can sense Sly seasoning his chops for what would be the Family Stone, and in the process helping prepare a couple of the future band members (his brother and sister) and an important collaborator (Billy Preston) for their work on major labels.

Some of Sly's early efforts show he was listening closely to, and borrowing some from, established rockers. His Autumn single "Buttermilk," says Alec, "was just a rip-off of the Stones' '2120 South Michigan Avenue' . . . and he'd quote 'Satisfaction' in other songs." His gifts as songwriter and arranger and as a tasteful blender of influences would blossom with the Family Stone, and he'd later return to producing others. For the time being, though, Sly wanted to follow Tom and Bob's footsteps in another direction, spinning discs rather than making them. He wasn't the only would-be celebrity to have applied a musician's skills to radio. Waylon Jennings, on KLLL in Lubbock, Texas, and B. B. King, on WDIA in Memphis, had also proven that they had the ears to detect potential hits, recognize catchy hooks, and understand what makes a pop song work. All three of these musicians were also able to apply their on-air experience to making their own listener-friendly music.

After training at the Chris Borden School of Broadcasting and graduating in 1964, Sly filled a slot on AM radio station KSOL, whose call letters announced its focus on soul and R & B, with some crossover to pop, aimed at a primarily black demographic.

Sly's speaking voice, like his singing, was strong and sensual, dipping, like Tom Donahue's, into a baronial lower register. His manner was hip and masterful, with many moments of humor and improvisation. Consider this broadcast bit of Sly's wily wisdom, copping from Shakespeare: "The whole world is a stage, and you only have a part to play, and if you don't play it right, you get kicked out of the party." And a warning, now easily assessed as prescient: "The Soul Brothers remind you to be cool," Sly intoned between hits. "Keep the poison out of the kids' reach. And keep it out of any fool's reach that might try to use it, you know what I mean? Keep it out of your woman's reach!"

"I love every one of them," he testified over the fade-out of the Supremes' rather inane soundtrack single "The Happening." "Especially Diana [Ross]. And she loves me! That's a gas," he opined, and after a signifying pause, he continued, "The movie, not the record." Any self-respecting Supremes fan would have seconded this assessment.

Radio execs and wiser listeners couldn't help but have realized that Sly knew his music very well. While KSOL hadn't KYA's national significance as a "break" station, Sly's broadcast presence there (he had the 7:00 p.m. to midnight slot), and later on the similarly formatted KDIA, bolstered his importance to the Bay Area entertainment scene, reaching beyond his black target audience to youth of other ethnicities. "Sly had a specific energy, he was clearly some kind of star," remembers Ben Fong-Torres, former *Rolling Stone* editor, ongoing rock historian, and current KFRC-FM "Classic Hits" radio personality. To the then-teenaged Ben, attending school and helping out in his parents' Chinese eatery in Hayward, Sly sounded "confident, but not smug . . . in kind of an 'older brother' sound, friendly, not coming on to anybody, not 'I am the disc jockey, so I am the king.'" The radio DJ's largesse was manifest in "the way he demanded requests and dedications and the way he talked to kids on the phone," making those conversations audible on-air.

"You would hear him bring in his instruments to the radio station and do his own station IDs," says Ben, about how creatively Sly carried out the obligatory identifications of his stations' call letters. "He would sing his commercials, he was so inventive, or he'd bring in his musician friends and do a little jam session. Back then, even though it was formatted, DJs could do things that were unique, more than what they can do today, which is nothing."

Pop writer Joel Selvin was a teenager back then, a white boy living in the Oakland ghetto with a job as a copy boy at the *San Francisco Chronicle*. Young Joel avoided KFRC, "where they played Herman's Hermits," in favor of KDIA, where Sly "was fast-talking, he was jivey, and he knew who the Beatles and Lord Buckley were, and so did I." Joel today recalls that "the other [KDIA] guys were like this old-fashioned black thing, being very carefully spoken and articulate, not necessarily sounding white but not sounding black. And Sly was laughing and squeaking and rhyming, it was an exciting thing. . . . And everybody remembers the dedications."

Joel observes that "this was a transitional period in the whole African American community, right? If you were older generation, you looked for a public persona that was presentable, decorous. There's some thinking that, because blacks were accorded second-class citizenship, in order to have a public face you had to be more white than white people." This impression was probably particularly strong in the Bay Area among those who, like the older

Stewarts, had relocated from regions of entrenched racism. But Sly, Joel believes, would have been well aware that "the old-fashioned thinking was going away with the young blacks, who were growing up at that time, and were assuming more independent postures." Sly's on-air independence was manifest more as cheeky subversion than as militancy or political diatribe.

Jerry Martini, whose sax services had helped put him close to Sly, used to listen on his car radio to Sly while on his way to a gig at the airport Hilton. When he had the chance, he'd visit his friend at the radio studio, where a small, unused piano sat against a wall. "So I suggested [to Sly], 'Why don't you just sing your whole show?' And it was a good suggestion," remembers Jerry. "He sang the news, he sang the weather." Sly would also mock the monotony of Bay Area weather by always announcing the temperature as "fifty-nine degrees," regardless of any actual deviation from that dreary norm.

The appeal and credibility of Sly's on-air sessions were further enhanced by occasional visits from his new friend Hamp "Bubba" Banks. They had become acquainted when the coif-conscious Sly became a patron at Bubba's Fillmore district hair salon, where the emerging radio personality perhaps came closer to acquiring "street cred" than at any other point before or after his celebrity. The neighborhood shop was favored by pimps, prostitutes, and young African Americans, and its proprietor was eager to promote himself over the airwaves. Bubba recalled for Joel Selvin that "I'd come on [the radio] and say, 'Sly, you come on and rap, I gotta go check my trap.' Just all this street slang." Banks, an ex-marine and sometime pimp himself, also shared the nocturnal bustle of North Beach with Sly and served as something of a hip mentor. "We became truly inseparable," Bubba recounted. "I would go to the [Urbano] house after we did our thing, and lay on the floor. Sly would smoke a little weed. But that was the extent of it." Bubba regretted having later exposed his younger friend to cocaine, but neither man seemed to have been making debilitating or addictive use of the drug during this earliest stage of their relationship. The constructive part of the alliance extended to Bubba's opening a club, Little Bo Peep's, where Sly acted as emcee and Rose, Sly's sister and later Bubba's wife, sold tickets.

Sly sought out yet more opportunities to do his own thing on the air. He found a copy of Ray Charles's great "Let's Go Get Stoned" in a garbage can, tossed there because of the seemingly illicit imperative in the lyric (which was actually to drink, not to drug), and started playing it, helping score yet another national hit for the man who'd helped inject soul into rock. Sly also deviated from the implicit color line of his stations' playlists. "They rarely played a white artist," notes Ben Fong-Torres about the Bay Area's black-identified stations. "Only the Righteous Brothers and certain sounds could make it on, blue-eyed soul with popularity. Sly was a bit broader than that; whatever he liked he'd put on." In among the Motown and Stax-Volt artists of the day, such as Otis Redding, Wilson Pickett, Smokey Robinson, Mary Wells, Marvin Gaye, the Supremes, Little Stevie Wonder, and the Temptations, he'd play the Beatles, the Rolling Stones, Bob Dylan, and white raconteur Lord Buckley, from whose pseudo-hip delivery Sly freely borrowed.

Sly's ascending career as a performing musician wasn't supplanted by his short career as a broadcaster; he kept gigging at a variety of local clubs. But "it's hard to do a hundred percent both ways," points out Sly's former KDIA colleague Chuck Scruggs. "He'd come in late and leave in a hurry . . . and I believe he left the station because he got so busy, he couldn't make his air schedule." Had Sly stayed in radio, "He probably would have developed his style. . . . He commanded an audience, because he was a people person, and he was [from] the community."

Bob Jones, another KDIA DJ, says that the station, for a while, held on to hopes that Sly would return to the airwaves someday after leaving them in 1966. But in any case, Bob is grateful for Sly's radio legacy. "Sly was absolutely good theater," says Bob. "He always had an opening and a closing, and the opening was dramatic. He was definitely an influence on me, and I was doing the same thing later: theater for the mind." Over the next couple of decades, though, on-air "personalities," black, white, or otherwise, who spun discs while ad-libbing their way into the ears and hearts of their listeners would gradually disappear from the dial.

Ria Boldway, finishing up at Vallejo High, stuck by Sly during those busy years when he was transitioning from school into multiple careers. During her senior year (1962–1963), Ria had started spending more time at the small place Sly had rented in Vallejo after moving out of his childhood home on Denio Street. She ultimately moved to San Francisco, accompanying Sly on some of his gigs with the Mojo Men. Of Sly's radio days, she remembers that "he was incredibly popular, as he was in high school. He was always one to show off, be lighthearted, and laugh his head off, and that's what he did on the radio as well." But Sly was also capable of being serious in an intimate setting. Ria had brought up marriage, and Sly had talked about having kids. "He said, 'Oh, we'll have the most beautiful little golden babies,'" she recalls. "Now, I'm a dark human being [of Mediterranean mien]. 'He'll never have golden babies with me,' I thought to myself. But instead of saying anything to him, I kept it to myself."

In one offhand moment, Sly told Ria, "I'm gonna get a blond wife and a white car and a white dog." She hadn't worried about the remark till Sly's attention began drifting away from her. Her regret came to a head one night when Sly bid her good-bye before taking off for a gig at the Condor. "I think I was still underage and couldn't go to some clubs yet," Ria says. "He'd gotten dressed and he got into a white Cadillac convertible with [the blond Condor waitress-turned-topless-icon] Carol Doda. And he went off. And I realized a whole lot of things then: that it was just not gonna happen, that we would not get married, as we had spoken of doing. He had other things on his mind; it was all career."

After that sad realization, "I talked to his mother and his father, and moped around the house for a while. I realized it was not gonna go anywhere. His mama didn't want it to anyway, 'cause she was afraid my father would kill him. She loved me and everything, like one of the little kids she took care of. She said, 'Just let him go and do what he needs to do.' And I did." Ria later left the country and married another man, but cherished her memories of her high school lover and would try to get close to him a couple of more times—after he'd launched himself into fame with the Family Stone.

Dance to the Music

— 1966-1968 —

Black and white, the young rebels are free
people, free in a way that Americans have
never been before in the history of their
country.

—ELDRIDGE CLEAVER
Soul on Ice

THE APPETITE FOR LIVE MUSIC in San Francisco in the late '60s supported an effervescent club scene in the North Beach neighborhood and beyond, where youthful talent could mature. Before deploying his considerable guitar skills around the city's clubs, Sly's younger brother, Freddie, had studied music in college for a short while and had been briefly employed by Billy Preston in Los Angeles. Signing on with future Santana vocalist Leon Patillo's Sensations, Freddie encountered a young drummer in the Excelsior district, who was sitting in with the Sensations during a downtown gig hosted by Sly in his radio star capacity. Just seventeen, Greg Errico (his Italian family name is accented on the second syllable) had already been playing beer joints for a couple of years. Freddie decided to include Greg in his own group, the Stone Souls.

"Freddie loved me," reflects Greg. "He was totally confident, he didn't look at color, he didn't look at age, none of that." Greg himself is modest about assessing his early worth, other than to say, "I did have very good ears, and I was musical as a drummer." His older brother, Mario Errico, who later became one of Sly's trusted lieutenants, is more forthcoming about what the brothers Stewart must have liked about Greg: "It was the way he played, for a white boy. He was funky, and he had this backbeat. They used to call him 'Hands-and-Feet.' I was proud as hell that my brother could play."

Greg and Mario's parents, Italian Americans who'd raised their sons to respect financial security and their imported 78-rpm recordings of Italian opera and popular music, were skeptical about their younger son's ambitions. "I said to Greg, 'I don't understand this,'" remembers Jo Errico, now in her mid-eighties. "And he said, 'Mom, you just wait. One day, you're gonna hear things I've played on, on the radio, and you're gonna maybe see me on television.' And we did! You had to give it to him; he pursued his dream."

Back in '66, the dream meant a booking with Freddie and the Stone Souls at Little Bo Peep's in the Excelsior, uniformed in slacks, shirts, and vests, backing such visiting acts as the Coasters when not performing covers of Wilson Pickett, Percy Sledge, and other pop-oriented soul material. Freddie was developing a tight rhythmic finesse, chopping out a crisp sixteenth-note chord style in the manner of James Brown band member Jimmy Nolen. Freddie's lead forays, though brief and economical, were executed with precision and taste on a variety of classy guitars, including the Fender Jazzmaster, Telecaster, Gibson SG, Gibson Les Paul, and—unusual for the time—a semi-acoustic (hollow body) Gibson

Byrdland. He'd never attain the status of a Clapton or Hendrix, but forty years later, Freddie was remembered by fans and rock writers as one of the Bay Area's influential guitar greats.

Back in April of '66, Freddie's group had earned a booking by former San Francisco Mime Troupe manager Bill Graham (the soon-to-be heavy-hitting rock impresario and godfather of the San Francisco sound) at a hall he'd been using, the Fillmore Auditorium, just west of San Francisco's Civic Center.

Meanwhile, Sly, after working with groups like the Continentals and the Mojo Men, formed the Stoners. (By this time, he'd adopted the surname "Stone" on-air). This group included Cynthia Robinson, a high-powered female trumpeter with a spunky stage presence, whom Sly had encountered on visits to Sacramento. Years later, Sly credited Jerry Martini with inspiring his formation of the Family Stone, an attribution which Jerry still cherishes. What's clear is that Jerry, on those visits to KSOL, began urging his musical friend to get off the air and on to a career with a new band. Sly was reportedly less than satisfied with his old group and wanted to form a new ensemble, while bandmate Cynthia just quit the Stoners in frustration. Looking ahead together, Sly and Cynthia checked out Larry Graham, a keyboardist and guitarist who had taken up the bass.

Like Sly, Larry was originally from Texas but had relocated as a toddler to Oakland, California, with his family. He'd drummed in his school band and had begun his musical career per se playing guitar, inspired by bluesmen like Clarence "Gatemouth" Brown, and had even sat in with a visiting Ike and Tina Turner. When Sly first heard him, Larry was gigging with his mother, Dell, a singer and pianist. That act had shrunk from a trio to a duo, requiring Larry to man both the organ and the guitar. When the organ broke down and the act still needed low registers, the resourceful Larry rented a St. George electric bass guitar to fill in. "I wasn't interested in learning the so-called correct overhand style of playing bass, because in my head I was going back to guitar, anyway," Larry later told *Bass Player* magazine.

The necessity of properly accompanying his mother inspired Larry's reputed invention of what has been variously called the slap-pop or thump 'n' pluck technique, later immensely influential on rock, funk, and jazz bassists. Most electric bassists up to that time had preferred the softer, rounder tones of conventional finger-style and picking methods. But Larry, as he described it to *Bass Player*, "would thump the strings with my thumb to make up for the bass drum, and pluck the strings with my fingers to make up for the backbeat snare drum," thus replacing two missing drums with one stringed instrument.

Sly and Freddie also assessed the talent manifest at each other's shows, and they frequented the Condor, where Sly's pal Jerry Martini was still blowing sax behind George & Teddy. Jerry incorporated the influences of soulful jazz giants Gene Ammons and Sonny Stitt. But he now says, "One of the reasons that attracted Sly to my playing was that I emulated [R & B innovator] Junior Walker more than any other white boy in town. Because [the others] were all trying to sound like Art Pepper." In effect, Sly needed a representative of the funky sass of Walker more than the post-bop jazz artistry of Pepper.

Greg Errico came to Urbano Drive in December 1966 for what he thought was another Stone Souls rehearsal. He describes the sequence of his knocking, Sly's mom, Alpha, opening the door, and the subsequent interchanges: " 'Where's Freddie?' 'Well, he's in the kitchen with Sly, eating chicken.' I went to the kitchen and looked around. 'Where's everybody, are we rehearsing tonight?' I said hi to Sly, he was the radio DJ. 'We're starting a new group tonight.

You wanna do it?' 'Well, I'm here.' I was just joking around. I was looking for the rest of the Stone Souls. But Sly was already looking out for one more attempt at what he had in mind." Greg later learned that he had actually been the second choice for drummer, after a failed attempt to recruit Bartholomew "Frosty" Smith-Frost, accompanist to Lee Michaels, a Hammond organ master popular around the Bay Area and later signed to A&M.

The group that assembled on that fateful afternoon on Urbano Drive to realize what Sly had in mind included brother Freddie, Greg Errico, Larry Graham, and Cynthia Robinson. There's no known recording of what went down in that basement, but it can be inferred, from what the players looked and sounded like on record and in live performance not all that much later, that it must have been thrilling and unprecedented in pop music.

Recalling the day for Joel Selvin, Cynthia noted that the musicians found Sly ready with "punching funky" arrangements of Top 40 songs, which he expected to later intersperse with his own original compositions in live sets. Larry, she says, raised a question about group leadership, which Sly met with an affirmation of his sole right to lead. (The potential for a standoff between these two persisted for years.) The group's name was a catchy mutation, with druggy undertones, of the pseudo-surnames both Stewarts had started performing under, as well as a statement of what would be the group's ethos, with Sly as unquestioned head of a tight-knit "Family."

The brand-new Family Stone's quest for a gig took them beyond the city limits and into the sights of the enterprising Rich Romanello, a couple of dozen miles down the San Francisco Peninsula. A few years Sly's senior, Rich had grown up among fellow Italian Americans in San Francisco's North Beach and Marina neighborhoods, and then stepped up to his father's bar business.

Music was vital to Rich's club vision. For the jukebox at his dad's Morocco Room in San Mateo, south of the San Francisco airport, the younger Romanello insisted on selecting the discs himself. "The jukebox company would not buy a record until it was a hit," he points out, "but I'd put in songs that I thought would become hits, so I had the hottest jukebox in the area." Long before "Runaround Sue" scored for Italian American rocker Dion DiMucci in 1961, "The only place you could hear it was at the Morocco Room, or you'd have to wait for it to play on the radio."

Visits to Tom Donahue and Bob Mitchell's shows at the Cow Palace convinced Rich of the commercial power of live rock. On a mission to convert the Morocco Room "from a neighborhood cocktail lounge into a young hot spot," he began to feature live entertainment, leaning toward the R & B end of the rock spectrum. Emile O'Connor (called "Little E") and Wally Cox, two of his featured performers, talked Rich into managing them. "It was black entertainment, and a white Peninsula crowd," he says. "But if there were any blacks that came in, they were welcomed. We weren't segregated." Later, Rich was advised to audition a white act from San Francisco, the Beau Brummels. He remembers their try-out at the Morocco Room in 1964. "There were maybe four people in the place, and they set up and started playing, and that old hair on my arm goes up. And when the hair on your arm goes up, you got something. It was a big change, to go from saxophones and black singers to a white guitar sound. But I hired 'em."

Soon enough, "They said, 'Be our Brian Epstein,' and that got my attention, because [Beatles manager] Brian Epstein was my hero." Rich's second management venture prompted a visit to the Morocco Room by Tom Donahue and Sly Stone, who had already worked with the Brummels at Autumn Records. Rich subsequently got to observe Sly in action at the Cow Palace and in the studio. "He was a very cool, low-key individual," Rich remembers about Sly. He supposes that "maybe at that time, because of his growing, there might have been a little bit of insecurity," which maintained Sly's low-key presence. This belied the young producer's manifest talent: "He'd get up and play in the studio, and I knew he could play just about any instrument. You knew he knew what he was doing."

Parallel club-owning and management functions continued for Rich, as did the connection with Autumn Records. He booked the Warlocks, later to morph into the Grateful Dead, and the Tikis, later more famous (albeit briefly) as Harpers Bizarre. On a single Labor Day weekend in 1966, Rich's earnings for booking the Jefferson Airplane in resorts north of San Francisco exceeded his take on the Brummels' two hit records. He decided to invest that money in converting another club on the Peninsula, in Redwood City, formerly a venue for big-band acts such as Stan Kenton and Count Basie. "When I walked into the place, for some reason they were just playing 'Winchester Cathedral' [a quirky retro hit by the New Vaudeville Band]," Rich recalls. "And I said, 'This place has the feeling of a church. I'm gonna call it Winchester Cathedral.'"

Rich needed an energizing act to christen the Cathedral. Walking down Broadway, the neon-lit strip in San Francisco's North Beach neighborhood, he encountered Jerry Martini, who had accompanied George & Teddy on a Morocco Room booking. "I've opened a new club in Redwood City," Rich told Jerry.

"Well, I'm with Sly," said the saxophonist, who was still psyched from the recent Urbano Drive conclave. "Sly put a new band together."

"You're kidding!"

"No, you've gotta hear us."

Rich was summoned to the Stewart family basement for the next rehearsal of the Family Stone. "I'm walking down the stairs, and I hear it," he recounts. "And that hair goes right up on my arm. I go, 'Oh shit, does this sound good!' And I go and sit down. They're just starting, but they're good. They were doing everybody else's music, they hadn't gone out on their own yet, but what they were covering was better than the originals, no doubt about it. Freddie singing 'Try a Little Tenderness'? Whew! They could play! So I hired 'em that night."

The Cathedral and its opening act, Sly & the Family Stone, were aggressively promoted by Rich through newspaper and radio advertising. He assumed there might not be widespread familiarity with radio jock Sly as a musician. On opening night—December 16, 1966—there was a long line to get into the new club. And there was plenty for the patrons of the early show, many of them teens, to smile about as they looked around after entering. "The whole place was red-flocked wallpaper, crystal chandeliers, and it had a real elegance about it," says Rich, about the design elements he'd retained from the previous owners. He'd added a stained-glass display inside a planter box, spelling out L-O-V-E. "We were capturing a little of the Haight-Ashbury, but this was not a hippie place. And if you look at [later] photographs of the Cathedral, kids dancing, you can see how appropriately dressed they are, for the time."

Both the dancing teens and the older sit-down crowd who took their place for the after-hours session, starting at about 2:00 a.m., seemed delighted with the brand-new Family Stone band, and the feeling seemed mutual. In subsequent bookings, on regular Friday and Saturday nights during the first half of 1967, the band took to opening its shows with the Spencer Davis Group's recent hit, "Gimme Some Lovin'," repeating the appreciative message, "So glad you made it!" "If you talk to the kids," says Rich, referring to the Family Stone as if they still were the youngsters he shepherded, "they might tell you it was the best place they ever played, for their own entertainment and satisfaction. . . . And that was probably some of the best they ever sounded."

Sly had taken notice of what Rich had done as manager of the Beau Brummels, and he approached the club owner about assuming that function for the Family Stone. Rich recalled his Brummels experience in a less positive light, but ultimately gave in to Sly's request. Word got around that bookings at the Cathedral alongside the Family Stone could help launch other new acts, including the young Santana Blues Band from San Francisco's Mission district. "I gave Carlos seventy-five dollars a night, and I gave Sly a hundred, 'cause I was the manager and had to get my commission." Rich remembers. The audience paid about two dollars a head to see this pre-legend double bill.

In the early months at the Cathedral, repeat customers were delighted with the Family Stone's creative covers of material from the soul and R & B side of the rock spectrum. "We did things like 'Shotgun' and 'Try a Little Tenderness,'" says Jerry Martini, "because we'd worked out a show thing where we'd walk around the room, dancing and playing tambourines." Larry's baritone voice effectively channeled Lou Rawls's on the soulful "Tobacco Road" and "The Shadow of Your Smile." "But we started immediately adding original songs, one by one," Jerry continues. "We even practiced dialogue, a little acting. I remember Freddie and Larry on a [Sly-penned] song that Larry sang, called 'Let Me Hear It from You.' They would talk to each other and say, 'I heard my girlfriend's gonna break up with me, but I wanna hear it from you.' It went over really well, personal life things." (The song was later included on the band's debut album, *A Whole New Thing*, but

43

without the dramatic spoken intro.) Jerry's commitment to the new group involved major changes in his own personal life, including forsaking a lucrative engagement with another band and moving in with his wife's family to minimize costs.

The Family Stone's extended engagements in Redwood City ultimately benefited both club and band, until the latter began to outgrow the former. In his management function, Rich booked the band into other clubs around the Bay and sought out larger show-cases. He put out an invitation to Bill Graham, now on his way to rock regency as owner and operator of San Francisco's Fillmore Auditorium, one of a handful of concert halls attractive to the bur-geoning crop of flower children who had cash to spend on tickets. Witnessing the band in action, Bill expressed little interest in its dance-inducing appeal, despite his previous year's booking of Freddie's band. Rich reacted with resentment. "I said, 'Bill, you probably have one of the best dance floors in all of Northern Cal-ifornia. But you've got all the hippies in their Indian squats, sitting on that floor like a bunch of vegetables. Do you think you ever want to get these people up and dancing?' Nope. Not ready. So we parted company. And after the session was over, Sly came up and said, 'Why not?' And I told him the story. He said, 'I'll change the music!' I said, 'Don't!' We stuck to our guns and said, 'Fuck Gra-ham and his psychedelic heads, we're on this path and we're stay-ing on this path.'"

Rich turned to a list of contacts he'd maintained while work-ing with Autumn Records, and picked out Chuck Gregory, the local promotion manager for Columbia Records. Chuck had secured Columbia's first rock act (Moby Grape), as well as a recording of Carol Doda and her backing band at the Condor. For Aretha Franklin, performing at a private party downstairs from the club, Chuck had recruited Sly and some other Condor familiars as backing musicians. Chuck then called Columbia's New York office, at Aretha's request, to propose recording the rising soul diva with Sly and the others. This promising project, conjoining two future superstars, never came to be: Columbia, ready to divest themselves of Aretha, gave it the thumbs-down.

On the night Chuck came to the Cathedral to assess the Family Stone, at Rich's invitation, in March 1967, "Everything that could go wrong went wrong," says the club owner. "Microphones went out, amplifiers went out, strings broke on guitars, it was just a fucking mess." Chuck's reaction came as a relief: "I think we got something." Inspired by this interest, Rich set about cleaning up his star act. "Sly had been in trouble with the IRS and the Musicians' Union," he says, "so we got his back dues straightened out and brought in Sid Frank, my dad's accountant." The band was sent to Don Wehr's Music City in San Francisco to equip itself with proper instruments and amplifiers, and then was sent across town to the trendy Town Squire for outfits. "They came out looking like fucking clowns," laughs Rich. "Jerry with his polka-dot shirt and Sly with his knickers. I said, 'What the fuck is going on?' But Sly was right, I was wrong. They were gonna be new, they were gonna be unique, their music was different, they were on their way."

Eye-catching fashion and coiffure remained hallmarks throughout the band's existence and into Sly's career beyond. The bandleader would go so far as to create outfits instantly with a rug and a knife. Though Hendrix's Experience had their towering Afros, Jim Morrison his tight leather pants, and Janis Joplin her hippy bell-bottoms, the Family Stone's group image of garish costuming almost seemed to prefigure the '70s—there were high-heeled boots, tight slacks or dresses, luminescent puffy shirts evocative of some gilded age, oversize hats atop oversize dos, and ornate jewelry. In publicity shots, on record covers, and in live performance, the band manifested a new standard of rock royalty.

Back in New York, Chuck Gregory's superiors at Columbia Records were still bedecked in three-piece suits and ties, smoking tobacco copiously while attempting to stay ahead of rapidly changing trends in music. An enthusiastic phoned dispatch from Chuck reached the ears of David Kapralik, who'd lateraled from his position in national promotions for Columbia (succeeding the notorious rock hater Mitch Miller) to managing A & R (artists and repertoire) for Columbia's rock-centered Epic Records. "Now that you're there [at Epic]," Chuck urged David, "come on out and I'll sign a hell of a band for ya." While still at Columbia, David had resurrected the legendary Okeh label and engaged performer and producer Curtis Mayfield and others to broaden the label's R & B catalog. He'd also coined the term "pop gospel" and had signed Peaches & Herb to Epic. Chuck's report about a black DJ with a racially integrated ensemble intrigued David, then in his early forties, and he flew out to San Francisco and slept off some of his jet lag at Chuck's home in Marin County, across the Golden Gate Bridge. "Then we woke up at 12:30 [a.m.] and took a cup of coffee," says Chuck. "My wife drove us down [to Winchester Cathedral] and Sly went on at two o'clock."

"I heard this sound that totally blew me away," remembers David. "And after the gig, probably about four in the morning, Sly and I went to a nearby International House of Pancakes, and we sat there looking at each other." From his current refuge on Maui, he can't recapture verbatim what transpired, but the grandiloquent David prefers to cast it in a "mythopoetic" format, inspired by his Jewish upbringing. "I just know that we made a connection in the magic mirror," he says, and he elaborates on the quality of this new relationship: "The nearer, the dearer, the clearer you see, Shema Yisrael Adonai Eloheinu Adonai Echad." Taken from Deuteronomy, this incantation means, "Here, Israel, the Lord our God, the Lord is One."

Aside from the insights into oneness inspired by Sly at the IHOP, David let the ambitious young artist know that he was intent on signing the band to Epic. The pair spent more time together over the next several days and nights, cruising around the Bay Area in Sly's ride. "He had to get to know me," David explains. "He was a street-wise kid. I'm not a street-wise kid. For better or worse I come from Plainfield, New Jersey, a middle-class situation."

Whatever Sly may have shared with David apparently didn't include any information about the prior management arrangement with Rich Romanello, who remembers Sly confronting him during this period. "He came back and said, 'I spent a lot of time with David, and I think I'm gonna do a deal,'" recounts Rich, who was made to feel "like someone had cut off my arm." Rich was offered a percentage of Sly & the Family Stone's future earnings, and was thus persuaded to release his client from his management contract. A new contract was promptly consummated by David in the basement of the Stewart home on Urbano Drive. "I said, 'Sly, I know I can help you fulfill all your dreams as an artist,'" remembers David. "Somehow or other I knew the power of my enthusiasm. I had total confidence." This prompted his return to the Epic offices in New York, where "I had that buzz happening. And when I have a buzz, I infuse that buzz in other people." It had worked in promoting the young Barbra Streisand early in the '60s. "I was a madman! I'd jump on desks, I would go in the middle of meetings, I would go into an office and climb on my boss's desk and have a demo in my hand and put it on the turntable. And that's also how I got attention for Sly in the beginning."

Back on the San Francisco Peninsula, the Family Stone completed its booking at the Cathedral in June '67, on the eve of the Summer of Love. Rich, despite what he'd been promised, saw no more money from the band. A couple of months later, the Cathedral was shut down by a fire, and its proprietor began contemplating a more dependable and rewarding occupation. His former star opening act had started looking east.

SLY & THE FAMILY STONE had a sense early on that they wouldn't be comfortable in anyone's pigeonhole. They were impressed by new manager David Kapralik's industry credentials and track record, but skeptical about following in the footsteps of his latest successful clients, Peaches & Herb, a successful lounge act with a few hits. "That's what [David] wanted us to be," notes Jerry Martini. "But Sly didn't wanna do lounge. He wanted to do concerts. So it was harder to break us."

Likewise, the Family Stone didn't hear itself as necessarily concordant with the hippie lifestyle and the so-called San Francisco Sound that accompanied it. "Being in San Francisco in 1967, it wasn't about rock 'n' roll, it was about psychedelics," says Greg Errico. "It was Quicksilver [Messenger Service], the Grateful Dead, Blue Cheer. And it had nothing to do with what we were doing, and we had nothing to do with that . . . I had no interest in going with a psychedelic group. What I found myself in the middle of, I couldn't have dreamed it any better. I felt very comfortable, very natural." What separated the Family Stone from many of the groups associated with psychedelia was its tightly plotted balance of voices and instruments, memorable on later hits. Many of the players involved in the San Francisco sound, by contrast, were guitar-based, with a more relaxed approach to songwriting and arranging that allowed for some amount of extended improvisation. These were the antecedents of today's jam bands.

The Family Stone needed a showcase away from San Francisco. With help from a Bay Area mover and shaker with gaming connections, they got an extended booking in July 1967 at a Las Vegas strip club called the Pussycat a Go-Go, which provided live entertainment (and only a bit of gaming) into the wee hours. By this point, the Family Stone, with David's consent, was playing original material alongside its innovative covers. Commuting between Vegas and Columbia's studio in Los Angeles on days off from the Pussycat, the band recorded some of the material for what would become *A Whole New Thing*. Sly's youngest sister, Vaetta (nicknamed "Vet"), provided background vocals, as she would for future albums, alongside Elva "Tiny" Mouton and Mary McCreary, two women with whom Vet had been performing and recording gospel as the Heavenly Tones.

The members of the Family Stone began to sparkle on and off the stage during their weeks in Vegas. Sly, Freddie, and Larry cruised the Strip in garishly colored Thunderbirds. Band members sometimes wore wigs for their Pussycat shows, and energized the audience by stepping down among them from the stage. Celebrity fans curious to witness the new music after their own gigs in the casinos included Bobby Darin and the Fifth Dimension. Ultimately Sly attracted a different kind of attention by taking up with the club owner's white girlfriend, Anita, provoking not only the expected sexual jealousy but a barrage of threats and racial epithets. Jerry related Sly's reaction: "[He] got up onstage and put his hands up and told the story to the people, and blew the club owner's mind. He said, 'We are gonna pack up and leave, because I can't have my woman here, and we are being racially persecuted' . . . Everybody that was at that club stood up and gave us a standing ovation." Jerry then had to hurriedly gather his then-wife and kids and join a police-escorted caravan headed out of town.

In the meantime, the tracks the band had laid down in L.A. for Columbia weren't leading to the rapid recognition they'd hoped for. *A Whole New Thing* "was a musicians' album," reflects Jerry. "So it never really made it big anywhere except Las Vegas, where we played. We didn't have a hit single, we had more of a cult following."

"The first album was just a labor of love, it was us," adds Greg. "We thought we were the greatest thing since spaghetti, but the only people who had [the album] were musicians. You'd go across the country and every musician had it under his arm, but nobody else knew about it."

Among his CBS colleagues and clients in New York, David was delighted to find *A Whole New Thing* making an impression on notable ears. "Its marketability I wasn't sure of," he admits. "But guys like Mose Allison and Jon Hendricks [were] talking about Sly. I heard this through Teo Macero, who produced them. 'He's a musicians' musician' was the word around CBS." David encouraged the band members to spend some time making a name for themselves in New York City, and they were up to the challenge.

"New York either loves you or they hate you, and we were a success there," Jerry reports. He remembers, during an early New York engagement, "having to take the subway from 136 West 55th Street, the Gorham Hotel, all the way down into the Village, wearing my weird clothes. People leave you alone, if you're weird in New York, they don't bother you."

In August '67, the act was booked at the Electric Circus, a venue operated by former talent agent Jerry Brandt, and among the invited guests was Al DeMarino, an up-and-comer at the William Morris Agency, where Brandt had been his boss. "Jerry called me up and said, 'I have this great band coming in, and I'm trying to do a favor for a friend, try to get down here and see them,'" Al remembers. "It was at the time when psychedelia had really started to come forth, and [the Circus] had become a very hip, 'in' place to be, with strobe lights and projections. I got there the first night. I was knocked out by the show, and immediately went up to Sly and the band and introduced myself. Jerry arranged an immediate meeting with David Kapralik . . . and I was very aggressive not only about signing them, but caring about them." What made Al so eager to secure the relatively unknown act for his employer, the largest diversified talent agency in the world, was, "The dynamics of the music, the strength of the music, Sly's leadership qualities onstage, and the chemistry within the band. They were more than band members, it felt like a family, they cared about each other."

Al perceived *A Whole New Thing* as "a smash record," but he shared David's doubts about its marketability. Whatever its mass appeal, the album displayed the sophistication of good jazz. Sly's sophisticated arrangements showcased Larry's articulate bass lines and the brassy teamed horns of Cynthia Robinson and Jerry Martini, all especially notable on the opening track, where "Underdog" quoted "Frère Jacques" in a minor key. Greg's drumming on that same track seemed to presage the hip-hop of thirty years later. The swirling segue from "I Cannot Make It" to "Trip to Your Heart" was pure '67 psychedelia. But this mix of elements rendered it difficult to categorize the album within the accepted format of radio playlists and record store bins.

Like the Jefferson Airplane with Grace Slick, and Big Brother with Janis Joplin, the Family Stone suggested a flower-power female-and-male bouquet from California, but they had a better handle on time and sounded more like a full-fledged band working and playing in harmony. They laid down pop grooves as impressive as Motown's, but without the impersonal grooming and choreography that glossed many of the faceless studio musicians who backed Berry Gordy's Motown vocalists. Onstage Sly Stone could sing with some of the bluesy grit and edge of Otis Redding and Wilson Pickett, but he also conveyed that endearing attitude of mischief that had once entranced both Ria Boldway and his radio audiences.

Sly's group also boasted the squalling brass and syncopated power of James Brown's, but without Brown's cold control of meter and melody and his autocratic approach to organization. The Godfather of Soul had been known to slap fines on band members who missed beats or hit wrong notes. But Freddie Stone told *Guitar World* magazine that in the Family Stone, "No one was held to any rules. It wasn't necessarily about playing the traditional guitar part or the traditional bass part or the traditional horn line. It was about giving the musicians the freedom to create a part that they thought was appropriate."

But the uniqueness of the Family Stone, however much it may have been appreciated in 1967 by members of the band and other musicians, didn't immediately result in strong records sales and a wide fan base. Clive Davis, then president of Columbia Records, which owned Epic, recalled for *Vanity Fair* magazine an early lunch with Sly. "I told him, 'I'm concerned that the serious radio stations that might be willing to play you'—by which I meant the underground FM radio stations—'will be put off by the costuming, the hairstyles.' . . . Sly said, 'Look, that's part of what I'm doing. I know people could take it the wrong way, but that's who I am.' And he was right. I learned an important lesson from him: when you're dealing with a pathfinder, you allow that genius to unfold."

Jerry Martini was summoned with Sly to meet with other Columbia execs and A & R (artists and repertoire) personnel responsible for artist development. "They played us other things, like [sweet soul successes] the Fifth Dimension, and they said, 'We want you to do this,'" Jerry recalls. "Sly walked out of there very disturbed and upset, because [of the lack of recognition of] his innovative ideas and drumbeats."

Greg remembers that, after the disappointment of *A Whole New Thing*, "Sly was very conscious that we had to simplify the music, that we had to find a subject that could talk to the audience. It was kind of like the Pied Piper . . . something that he had to touch upon, and live with himself, because he was going to have to be doing 'it' every night. We were all gonna have to do 'it' every night."

David Kapralik recalls Sly "coming into my office and saying, 'I'm going back to San Francisco. And I'm gonna stay there. And if anything ever happens with [the debut] album, let me know about it.' And I say to him, 'Sly, you gotta make a hit single. And you have to have a dum-dum-repeat lyric. And in between all those dum-dum-repeats, you put all your *schticklach*.' That was my first and only A & R suggestion to him in all the years that we were together. Because I'm not qualified, I'm not a musician. That was just something I knew from being a promotions man all those years."

Sly reportedly sought a transfer to Atlantic Records, the legendary R & B, soul, and jazz label whose roster included Ray Charles and the Coasters, but he demurred when Atlantic asked him to forsake his band for their hand-picked musicians. (It wouldn't be the only time that a label tried to break up the band; it would happen again around the recording of *Riot*.) Sly was not only insistent on maintaining the Family Stone, but on enhancing it with his middle sister, Rose, whom he approached on his return to San Francisco. "I didn't want to just be a slave to the keyboard," Rose admitted later in *The Skin I'm In*. "And [Sly] said, 'No, you can just sing.' I said, 'Okay, then.' So I quit my job [at a San Francisco music store] and the next thing he said was, 'Okay, we got you on keyboards.' I was so mad!" Fortunately for the band and fans alike, Rose also got to display her clarion soprano as the group's lead female vocalist. Her sound partnered gorgeously, and uniquely, with Sly's funky midrange and Larry's soul-stirring bass-baritone vocals

These days, without having scored a blockbuster at the start, an act like the Family Stone might well be dropped from any major label. In the late '60s, new acts were still being given a chance to develop their style and realize their artistic and commercial potentials. By the fall of '67, Al DeMarino was touting Sly & the Family Stone "within the agency at every opportunity, even at TV meetings and film meetings," and finding what bookings he could for them. "What I felt I needed to do in that initial year was select sizeable, worthwhile engagements," he says. But that "was easier said than done, because with any new act you're up against people who don't want to pay you what you're worth. So you bang the drums."

Propelled by Al's and David's metaphorical drumming and Greg's literal efforts, a much more accessible sophomore album, *Dance to the Music*, was assembled in New York's CBS recording studios. Don Puluse, an engineer young in years but musically well trained (at Eastman and the Manhattan School) and adept at deploying the then-new eight-track technology, was assigned to record the bulk of the album in September 1967. (A couple of tracks had been recorded in California earlier by Bryan Ross-Myring.) But aside from electronics, Don first needed to recharge his young clients' energy for the project.

"I had to give them a bit of a pep talk, because of the downers of Atlantic Records and CBS, where you had people already knocking them before they had even laid down anything," Don recalls. "I had to say, 'Hey, guys, you put all that aside. You're in the studio now, now is the time to make a record. We can't worry about what the suits in the other building are worrying about.' And Sly said, 'Yeah, sounds right, man, let's go!' And they went in there, and the thing which really stood out was the energy, which was outrageous. They would do very few takes, and to listen back they would come into the control room and dance."

The group's rightful reveling in their own music didn't interfere with the task at hand. "Sly would bark out orders: 'Jerry, do this! Cynthia, do that! Freddie, play it this way!' He would just, in about thirty seconds, summarize what he expected, and they'd be playing again. We did some overdubbing, but basically they did the whole take." Producer Don Was, in *Rolling Stone* in 2004, pointed out, "Sly orchestrated those early records in very advanced ways—a little guitar thing here that would trigger the next part that would trigger the next part."

Changes then in progress in the mode of studio recording may have furthered Sly's own tight control of the process, Don Puluse figures. "The groups had started coming in . . . saying, 'Hey, we're not gonna record with one guy and mix [i.e., process the recorded tracks] with another guy,'" he explains. "It wasn't like the old three- or four-track recordings, where they did everything at one time, did a little overdubbing, and sent it to a mix room." With more tracks to manage, "This was much more complicated. They would do overdubbing, over a period of weeks or months. Then, if they'd sent it to a new guy, he'd have to start all over. So I wound up [assigned to artists] like Sly, and later [the jazz-rock ensemble] Chicago, people who insisted on doing the mixing right there where they knew the sound, and with the same engineer." Don had the good taste to realize, with Sly's band, that "it would be foolish to try to get ultra-clean sounds, when what was really important was the music. I had done a lot of recording, but *Dance to the Music* had so much funk to it. Whoa! Where the hell did that come from? It was incredible!"

Funk had just begun to define itself within pop music in the late '60s, though its roots of course reached much further back. Funk and soul scholar and writer Rickey Vincent, in his *Funk: The Music, the People, and the Rhythm of the One*, singles out a definition of the form by Fred Wesley, a trombonist and collaborator with James Brown, Bootsy Collins, and George Clinton. Says Fred, "If you have a syncopated bass line, a strong, strong heavy back beat from the drummer, a counter-line from the guitar or the keyboard, and someone soul-singing on top of that, in a gospel style, then you have funk." The Family Stone had all of this, as well as an embarrassment of individual and collective uniqueness and talent. Jerry claims that Cynthia was "the first female African American trumpet player in history." While this is unsupportable—Valaida Snow, for one, launched a successful career on vocals and trumpet in 1918—it's evident that female instrumentalists, aside from occasional pianists and guitarists, were rare in rock, and that Cynthia had acquired a strong, spirited, and accurate horn technique in her hometown of Sacramento. "Cynthia," wrote Sly in *Dance to the Music*'s original liner notes, "is one of the most talented trumpets alive and that includes guys!" Jerry himself, who'd played Vegas and overseas venues before anybody else in the Family

Stone, was a sophisticated jazz-wise reedman. Together he and Cynthia often gave the impression of a much larger brass section.

Larry laid down his trademark down-and-dirty thumpin' and pluckin' bass, connected through new effects units designed for guitars—fuzz and wah-wah pedals, which altered the instrument's signal to give it a fat or stinging "underwater" tone. Larry's taut, snappy slaps of his Fender Jazz and Vox Constellation basses, making use of melody as rhythm, was a stimulating change-up from the happy bass burble of Paul McCartney or James Jamerson, and he influenced imitators for decades to come.

Freddie possessed, in the opinion of bandmate Jerry, "just about the most innovative guitar style of all. . . . You ask any of the modern-day rhythm guitarists who they listen to, and Freddie Stone, or Freddie Stewart, would be at the top of the list. There's no funkier or better rhythm guitar player."

His brother Sly, having willed the guitar function to Freddie, had quickly mastered a variety of keyboards, and was heard on both joyful and soulful organ passages throughout the album, with sister Rose partnering prettily on keyboards and solo and harmonized vocals. Sly variously made use of a Farfisa Professional, Yamahas of various years, a Vox Continental, and often a classic Hammond B-3. Greg powerfully and confidently propelled the rhythm, without encroaching on Larry's standout rumbles. "Greg had a drumming style that really complemented what I was doing," Larry testified to *Bass Player*. "We never had any collisions. It wouldn't have worked if he filled up a lot of space, which is what everybody else was doing at the time. . . . Greg plays on the money; he doesn't rush or lag."

It took the newly invigorated band a few months to get heard beyond 52nd Street. But when the second album's title tune was released as a single in the dawn of the new year, 1968, it took hold of the hearts, minds, and wallets of the general public on both coasts, in between, and around the globe. It climbed to number 8 on the *Billboard* pop chart and to number 7 in the United Kingdom. Out on the West Coast, "Dance to the Music" caught up with young would-be rock authority Joel Selvin on a blissful Saturday morning, while he was driving down the Eastshore Freeway near Berkeley with the radio on. "And it's Sly, sitting in on KDIA again," Joel remembers. "He hasn't been on in maybe a year. Wow, Sly! And he's all pumped up, as usual, and he's got his record, and he puts it on. . . . It was if something had come from outer space! It was so far beyond anything we had heard on the radio up to that point: the breakdown of the a cappella voices, the way the vocals were voiced, Larry Graham's boom-boom-boom, the way it was all pieced together. It was just literally the way I said in my book: There was black music before Sly Stone, and black music after Sly Stone. A watershed event, and that was the record."

Evocative of the congregational celebrations in which the Stewart children had performed on childhood Sundays, "Dance to the Music" inspired the primal directive of the tune's title, but also showcased the newly visible act in a manner unusual in rock and most other genres of pop music. Within the standard three-minute format of a radio single, individual instruments were introduced, a quote from Wilson Pickett's "Mustang Sally" was inserted in homage, and a couple of individual players (Cynthia and Jerry) were actually named in the lyric. Individualized voices were heard: Cynthia's raucous, spoken imperatives ("Dance to the music!" and "All the squares, go home!"), Larry's display of his matching bass vocals, and Sly's impresario tenor. The highlighting of each voice and instrument was almost pedagogical, like a rock band equivalent to Benjamin Britten's *The Young Person's Guide to the Orchestra*.

Just as at the Cathedral, this was a band to be listened to as much as danced to. The album's extended twelve-minute "Dance to the Medley" spawned not hits but catchy breaks, later to be highlights of live shows, not only for Sly & the Family Stone but much later for the group's twenty-first century spin-off bands. The three-part "Medley" encompassed stereo-spanning free-form interludes evocative of what was being evolved as mind-bending acid rock by groups like the Jimi Hendrix Experience, the Jefferson Airplane, and the Doors.

"It touched people more than I ever thought it would," says Greg about the *Dance to the Music* album. "It was a process of the whole group. And we were able to do it in a way that you got respect from your peers, other musicians, and you could talk to the average cat on the street. Everybody dug it—black, white. . . . Even to us, it was like, if you just be honest, and give it all you have to give, it will pay off." The band's manifest belief in racial harmony and sexual equality, more explicit in later lyrics, was touched on in a couple of tracks, "Color Me True" and "Don't Burn Baby."

The payoff for both the honesty and the talent became abundant as the Family played shows on both coasts over the course of 1968. "The biggest thrill was, the first time you heard that record on the radio, it felt so good," says Greg. "You go to a city, you get in the rental car, you turn the radio on, the song comes on. That felt better than knowing you were selling a lot of albums." Freddie, testifying from his current perspective of a sober man of the cloth in *The Skin I'm In*, was tempted into an awkward smile. "We felt like we'd gone on some kind of . . . I don't even want to say the word, but we were lit up," he confessed.

For those who witnessed the early concerts or bought the *Dance to the Music* album (and not just the single) when it was released later in 1968, the Family Stone was something to see as well as hear. In the album's cover and publicity photos and onstage, and in its TV appearances that year, the biracial makeup of the outrageously outfitted group was as impressive as was its mix of genders. To his credit, Sly never proffered Rose or Cynthia, both very attractive women, as background eye candy, as Ray Charles had with his Raelettes, but as integral members of the act.

"At a time of great social unrest in this country, this man came forth with an integrated band, the members of which got on famously, as brothers and sisters, and never had a problem anywhere they went," notes Epic's Al DeMarino. This feature broadened the band's appeal across racial lines in audiences and among older liberal-minded fans of Al and David Kapralik's generation.

David explains his personal perspective on race and American culture. As children in Plainfield, New Jersey, in the 1930s, he and his siblings had been "among the only Jews in our elementary school, and we were subjected to a lot of prejudice, and it was hurtful. . . . I didn't play with the other Caucasian kids, but during the lunch hour the Negroes, as they were called back then, took me in, and we related." As an aspiring Broadway actor in the next decade, David and black actress Jane White founded Torchlight Productions "to integrate Negroes into theater, movies, and the media." Switching to a day job at Columbia Records, David bonded with legendary producer John Hammond in bolstering the label's commitment to rhythm and blues, resurrected the Okeh label as a showcase for black music, and had, with Jerry Brandt, brought several swinging black acts to Columbia from Harlem churches. With this history of dedication, David was perhaps bound to hitch his star to what he thought he saw in the Family Stone and heard in the music created by its black leader. "I saw Sylvester as a vehicle for expressing, lyrically and socio-dynamically, his bringing the races together at this juncture in history," declares David. Sly's own high hopes were not quite so altruistic.

Everybody: Stand!

— 1968–1970 —

Music is a higher revelation than all wisdom and philosophy, it is the wine of a new procreation, and I am Bacchus, who presses out this glorious wine for men and makes them drunk with the spirit.

—LUDWIG VAN BEETHOVEN

Nothing is more singular about this generation than its addiction to music.

—ALLAN BLOOM, AMERICAN PHILOSOPHER

THE SEEDS OF FAME FOR SLY & the Family Stone had been planted, but it took a while for the band to reach extravagant blossom. A third Epic album, *Life*, was recorded in May 1968, while the band was still sampling its *Dance*-driven success. A new kind of confidence was perceptible in the LP's opening track, "Dynamite!," which engineer Don Puluse says was tangible in the studio. Confidence notwithstanding, nothing on

Life ever shared its predecessor's success, although in retrospect it's hard to hear why not. Several of the album's cuts, particularly "Fun," "Love City," "M'Lady," and the title piece, bear much of the trademark energy and listener-friendly impulsion of the group's earlier and later hits. The title cut opened with Sly imitating the sound of Laffing Sal, a mechanical clown from Playland at the Beach, San Francisco's erstwhile amusement park. This helped set the tone of the track's (and the album's) life-is-a-circus sentiments, reflective of the good vibes the band was still enjoying. *When I party, I party hearty*, the band declared in "Fun," and blasts of horns from Jerry Martini and Cynthia Robinson helped celebrate the sentiment, which took in family members—brother, sister, daddy, and momma—and a trademark canny commandment to the congregation of fans: "*Socketh unto others / As you would have them socketh to you.*"

Larry Graham led the exuberant "M'Lady" with some of the bassist's fattest, fuzziest runs heard to date, augmented by Freddie's fast, chunky funk chording and Jerry's giddy clarinet. The bassist's thump-'n'-pluck style had grown more fluid, and his lines on various of these tracks, notably "Dynamite!," would be adapted into innumerable disco bottoms boogieing over dance floors in the '70s. Record sales indicated that the public was not yet buying into all this artistry and delight, but they would with *Stand!*, the fourth album, whose several singles began bombarding the hit parade the following year.

Over the relatively brief period of gestation of its first three albums and of the public's reaction to them, Sly & the Family Stone were transformed from best-kept secret to an inflating commercial success. Along the way, on the road between coasts, the band was less recognized and more challenged. "I remember that Sly and I drove the equipment truck," says Jerry, "and Daddy [Sly's father K. C. Stewart] followed behind us in a huge station wagon. Drivers changed every hundred miles or so. Sly and I changed when we felt like it, [but] I usually drove and Sly wrote [music]. We talked lots, which kept us awake. These were great times, when there was not very much hard drugs. We enjoyed wine, a few drinks, and some weed, but not too much, as it makes you too tired to drive.

"There were no roadies at first, the band was the roadies," Jerry continues. "Daddy was the road manager. We learned the hard way how to read maps correctly. The straight line is not the fastest when it comes to highway travel. We learned it was so much faster to take the Ohio Turnpike and major highways, as opposed to driving through some scary backwoods towns."

The larger community of Detroit, where racial tension had erupted in 1967, provided its own drama. "There were riots going on, there was a curfew, it was three in the morning, and we got lost in the back streets somewhere," Greg remembers. "And all of a sudden the National Guard pulls us over. And here they look in the van, and it's black and white hippies, and that's challenging. But when they pull us out and line us up, Sly starts mouthing off, not accepting certain things. We didn't have any weapons, [but] we're up against the wall, they have machine guns, there's a race riot going on, and this is a very tense situation. And [Sly is] treating it like it's Sunday afternoon: 'Don't say anything, 'cause you're gonna hear it back from me.' That was challenging to the point of dangerous, and we're literally yelling at him to back off." In Greg's opinion, this incident (and others like it) was less a reaction of the authorities to the band's racial makeup than to its leader's personality, "'cause he had a very sharp and defined attitude about what he represented and what he was saying. I think that challenged more people than just the fact that he was black."

Back in New York, the group relished the satisfaction of being presented by Bill Graham, who a year earlier had refused to book them at his influential Fillmore Auditorium in San Francisco. In March 1968, the West Coast impresario had opened the Fillmore East in New York's East Village, and a few months later, he received a call from Epic's Al DeMarino. "Rumor was afloat that Jimi Hendrix was coming in," Al recalls. "Now, Bill Graham, at Fillmore East and West, had a three-act format: opening act, supporting act, headliner, and would very seldom think of deviating from that. So I called Bill . . . and I said, 'Look, why don't we try this: why don't we have a hundred-percent-equal star billing. Below Jimi, special guest star: Sly & the Family Stone.' He said, 'Let's go with it!'"

What they'd created was a night to remember in rock history, with classic comparisons and contrasts. Both Sly's Family and Jimi's Experience were multiracial bands led by charismatic black men, but Jimi's music at this point was much more blues-based, though he'd soon find that approach restrictive. Jimi was having to contend with the reputation he'd created as "The Wild Man of Pop," prompting audience expectations of his guitar acrobatics, inverting the instrument, licking the strings lasciviously, and maybe destroying the guitar onstage, all the while coaxing hallucinogenic wails of feedback from stacks of amplifiers. It may have challenged Jimi that Sly and his up-and-coming act were being perceived more as entertainers and musicians than as a psychedelic freak show. This contrast may have helped influence Jimi, in his last years, to turn away from the pure guitar theatrics that helped launch his career and move toward the more soulful palette displayed on *Electric Ladyland* and *Band of Gypsys*.

"And what Sly did, the first show on that Saturday night," Al reminisces about the Fillmore face-off, "he literally marched the band off the stage [while doing the hambone], through the aisles, and marched the entire audience out onto Second Avenue before the second show was about to begin. . . . Traffic had to be halted for about an hour." In addition, Jimi had to allow for a forty-five-minute interlude instead of the usual twenty-minute break before he took the stage, to give the crowd enough time to cool down.

During a period where he and Jimi were dating the same woman, Al had a chance to assess the guitar legend's personal take on Sly. "I think there was some competitive spirit within," says Al, "but I know there was great respect. . . . I know that [Jimi] admired Sly's music and wanted to go beyond the power trio [the configuration of his Experience act."

The Family Stone's reputation for eye-and-ear-filling enter-tainment justified a booking in London in September 1968. But hints of troubles to come ended up dooming the mini-tour. Sly refused to begin one show when he was offered what he considered an inadequate substitute for his own keyboard, delayed in transit. Then Larry Graham got busted for possession of a joint, which he'd taken from Jerry, despite Jerry's warning to dispose of it before passing through customs. The flustered group returned to the States and to the recording of the optimistic "You Can Make It If You Try," the earliest track of what would become the fourth album, *Stand!* Production of the record continued on into the first part of 1969, with the band shuttling between New York and San Francisco, partly to work at the latter's Pacific High Recording Studios and partly for the Stewart siblings to keep in touch with their genetic family and its local church.

The first hit off the new album, released in April '69, was "Everyday People," an anthem in which Sly clearly stated that *My own beliefs are in my song*, seemingly inspired by the ethos of '60s San Francisco. Referencing awareness of the era's variety of race, class, and lifestyles—*different strokes for different folks*—the song maintained that *I am no better, and neither are you / We are the same whatever we do.* Larry sustained a one-note pulse under the message, later telling *Guitar World*, "I'd never done that before. . . . That's where the freedom of creativity came in for the band, that we'd be allowed to do that." The song's sentiments matched the hopes of the generation they were aimed at, to expand and maintain egalitarian ideals and tolerance. And with this song, the band, which seemed to be not only singing about these hopes but actually living them, was rewarded with its first-ever place at the top of the pop hit singles chart, for a month.

The title track, "Stand!," was the next to land on the charts, though not as high. It opened with a dramatic roll from Greg Errico and featured yet another of Larry's powerfully percussive bass figures. In a rare move, the coda for this song was recorded separately by Sly with studio musicians after he decided it needed more brassy drama, befitting its lyrical declarations: *You've been sitting much too long / There's a permanent crease in your right and wrong* and *There's a midget standing tall / And a giant beside him about to fall.* Sly was beginning to distinguish himself among pop songsmiths for the subtlety, imagination, and sometime humor of his music writing as much as for his musical virtuosity. "You could hear the songs getting stronger, the melodies getting stronger," Larry told *Guitar World.* " We were becoming a better band, better musicians, and [Sly] was becoming a better writer."

Sly himself wielded the bass on "You Can Make It If You Try." The propulsive, intoxicating "I Want to Take You Higher" only made it to number 60 on the singles charts (on the flip side of "Stand!"), but it was to return to prominence later, on the strength of its inclusion on the set list at Woodstock.

The *Stand!* album itself, which reached number 13 on the *Billboard* pop charts in April '69, held experimentations and revelations beyond what was manifest in its individual chartable hits. They included Sly's use of the vocoder, an early synthesizer that had the effect of making his a voice sound like an eerie, trippy electronic instrument. The album's second track began with the dual advisory, *Don't call me nigger, whitey / Don't call me whitey, nigger.* This polemical reference to racism, very rare in Sly's lyrics, effectively blocked airplay, but the song highlighted Rose in a soulful plaint, partnered by Freddie's roiling wah-wah guitar. An atypically dense evocation of Hendrix-like blues rock, it sounded a rightful reaction to recent strife, including the assassination of Martin Luther King Jr. a year earlier. "Sing a Simple Song" broadcast a very different, sunnier sentiment in funky syncopation. The psychedelic blues instrumental "Sex Machine," at fourteen minutes, far outlasted most rock album tracks of the time, and prefigured the jam band format of coming years. Freddie reflected later that he'd rehearsed laboriously for this jam, but ended up being allowed to improvise on the spot.

Stand! contained yet more remarkable tracks and held on to the charts for over a hundred weeks. It served to solidify the Family Stone's unique synthesis of vocal-centered R & B with guitar-based rock. "Oh, man, that was the greatest—our greatest album, without a doubt," Freddie later opined to *Guitar World*. "It's my favorite because we were still fresh and hungry and sharp." If the band had disbanded at this point in time, it would have already scored a secure place in rock history.

Over what fans perceived as a long two years before the advent of another album, the Family Stone watched itself be illuminated and ultimately transfigured by the spotlight of success. Jerry commented on the peaks of this period for *The Skin I'm In*, saying, "The feeling that we'd gone Big Time made us feel really good. First-class tickets, limousines, instead of Sly and I driving the truck and Big Daddy in back with the van." How the band members moved through this phase of their youth was of course affected by their celebrity. Those who were married experienced strains on those bonds, and whether married or single, there were increasing opportunities for carnal indulgence, as referenced in *Life*'s final track, "Jane Is a Groupee": *She's got a thing for guys in the band / Every musician's biggest fan . . . Claps her hands, without a doubt / Has no idea what the song's about.*

There are reports of other females in Sly's life whom he may have considered more significant. The reunions with his first love, Ria Boldway, are accounted for later in this story. It appears that Anita, Sly's fateful companion from the Pussycat in Las Vegas, accompanied him to New York and on some of the group's early road trips. Stevie Swanigan, known as Stephani Owens when she was later interviewed by Joel Selvin, was brought in by David Kapralik in the fall of 1968 to work as secretary and personal assistant to Sly and the band. She revealed to Joel, "We had some intimate times, I will say that, but I was never [Sly's] girlfriend, I was more his conscience. I never took on the attitude of being his woman, because it would have made me less effective in the things I was supposed to do. . . . I was in and out a lot, because he wanted our relationship to be one where he could control me as another individual, as a woman. [But] I wanted him to respect me for what I could contribute, and for my mind."

Another perspective on Sly's love life appears in the pages of an autobiography by Deborah Santana, *Space Between the Stars*. Debbie, long married to (and more recently divorced from) guitar legend Carlos Santana, devotes a half dozen chapters to her early relationship with Sly. It had begun on the San Francisco street where Deborah, then known as Debbie King, lived, in the summer of 1969, with her parents, black jazz guitarist and bandleader Saunders King and his Irish American wife, Jo Frances. Sly, who'd been staying in his parents' Urbano Drive house nearby, stopped his vehicle in the middle of the street to make conversation with the attractive eighteen-year-old, eight years his junior, who had just a few weeks earlier viewed his televised appearance on *The Ed Sullivan Show*. By the time Sly and the band flew east in preparation for the Woodstock Music and Arts Fair a few weeks later, the teenager had begun an intense, long-term liaison with the rising rock luminary, and it lasted through the spring of 1972. (Stevie Swanigan's professional services to Sly began slightly sooner, but were more or less contemporaneous.)

Debbie's account provides a rare look at a period of Sly's personal life by an intimate insider. There are images of the Urbano Drive homestead, with Debbie petting one of Sly's earlier pet dogs, the Great Dane called Stoner, "while Sly played the piano, writing lyrics on yellow tablets and setting notes and chords onto staff paper." Debbie goes on to write, "Mama [Alpha Stewart] made the [rehearsing Family Stone] play softly because of the neighbors. Mama was usually in the kitchen cooking, or sitting at the table in the window, reading her Bible. She was sweet, with a twinkle in her eyes. Her heavy body moved slowly, and Sly danced around her, running back downstairs [to the basement], where she never went. I would sit with her and answer questions about my family and church."

Space Between the Stars goes on to describe Debbie's escape to New York with Sly, where they shared a courtly romance enhanced by marijuana and LSD. Debbie didn't follow the band to Woodstock, but saw Sly often, after she'd enrolled at California State College in Dominguez Hills and he'd relocated to a mansion in Coldwater Canyon in Los Angeles, not far away. She refers to Sly's sharing cocaine with her, to help her maintain her academic schedule. She also reports that by 1971, she'd dropped out of college, and that Sly's cocaine use drove him into occasional medical emergencies. Within a year, she writes, Sly had subjected her to a couple of episodes of physical abuse, and she'd left L.A. and their relationship, soon to start the study of yoga and a new romance with her future husband and rock-legend-in-the-making Carlos Santana.

A separate reflection of the benign glow in which Sly and Debbie had begun their affair is heard on Ben Fong-Torres's recording of an interview he conducted with Sly in Los Angeles in the fall of 1969 for the then-new *Rolling Stone* magazine. "Debbie's smart," Sly told the young reporter, "the brightest girl that has ever been associated with me in any way like this. She lived right around the corner from me and I didn't even know it. . . . I went to England and all over the place, all I had to do was go up the street and it would have been cool." The young lady in question was heard to reciprocate his esteem. "What Sly has in his head, he knows is right," she advised Ben, "so it doesn't excite him to read somebody who agrees with him."

A few months earlier, in July 1969, impresario George Wein expanded the lineup at his Newport Jazz Festival in Rhode Island by booking rock and blues acts along with expected jazz greats such as Art Blakey, Miles Davis, Bill Evans, and Rahsaan Roland Kirk. Among the youth-oriented bookings were Jeff Beck, Blood, Sweat & Tears, James Brown, B. B. King, John Mayall, Frank Zappa, and Sly & the Family Stone. The rock roster inevitably attracted a different, difficult demographic. On two successive nights, crowds breached the fences during the rock portion of the program, which on the second night featured Sly and company. George was billed for overtime law enforcement and replacement of the fence and was ordered not to book any more rock acts.

A month later, Sly & the Family Stone were among the cultural heroes invited to entertain a half million paying and (mostly) non-paying throngs of youth swarming over a bucolic farmstead in upstate New York.

THE WOODSTOCK MUSIC AND ARTS Fair was a point of mass affirmation for a generation heady with rebellion, experimentation, hedonism, and the occasional breaching of fences. In retrospect, it stands out as a showcase for a very healthy period in the development of American popular music. More than three decades later, youthful energy sparkled in the eyes of the now-middle-aged members of the Family Stone as they invoked the experience in the documentary *The Skin I'm In*. Greg recalled reveling with Janis Joplin at a nearby Holiday Inn, before his band's scheduled appearance on the early morning of August 17. Freddie reported that in the wee hours of their performance that Sunday, "It was dark when we went on, you could see nothing but candles. And, man, when the sun came up! We began to see how many people there were."

"When we got there, at three o'clock in the morning, we were tired, we were grouchy, we were all full of mud," added Jerry. "We got out there and looked at the audience, who were all in their sleeping bags, and when we started playing, they all jumped out of their sleeping bags. We felt the vibe between the audience and the band, and honest to God, all the hair on my arms stood straight up." Was this evidence of a reprise and validation of Rich Romanello's prophetic reaction to the band at its birth three years earlier?

Cynthia described the scene for *People* magazine: "It was pouring rain. Freddie got shocked. The equipment was crackling. But

Sly was like a preacher. He had half a million people in the palm of his hand." Larry told *Vanity Fair*, "It's like when an athlete like Michael Jordan realizes the extent of his gifts and goes, 'Oh, I can do that.'"

Michael Wadleigh's Oscar-winning documentary film about Woodstock (edited by a pre–*Mean Streets* Martin Scorsese) and the associated three-LP soundtrack served both as souvenirs of the generation's peak experience and as an extension of Woodstock's legend to those who couldn't, or wouldn't, be there. Sly & the Family Stone played one of the festival's best sets, including "M'Lady," "Sing a Simple Song," "You Can Make It If You Try," "Stand!," "Love City," "Dance to the Music," "Music Lover," and "I Want to Take You Higher," but only the last three made it onto the film and record. It's not the band's best performance, but it is one of their most celebrated, and the powerful current between stage and captive audience is tangible.

David Kapralik, though still managing the group, didn't witness the Woodstock gig until he saw the documentary. Now, with the benefit of hindsight, he views the indelible image of Sly, his arms raised in salute to the throng, with long white fringes trailing off the jacket, as a harbinger of hard times. "I knew that this was Icarus, his wings made of wax, and [the spotlight] was the sun he flew too close to," David opines. His characteristically visionary metaphor is drawn from Greek mythology, but he refers to a real-life meltdown that would increasingly weaken his bond with Sly, Sly's bond with the band, and David's hold on his own well-being.

On the surface, it looked like Sly & the Family Stone's career was in full flight, with the *Woodstock* film and recording helping to uplift and sustain the band's popularity. Without a new album in the works, though, Columbia decided to launch a couple of singles. The laid-back and jazzy "Hot Fun in the Summertime," released in August '69, rose to the number-2 spot on the charts in the fall of that year; early in 1970, "I Want to Take You Higher" was released as the A-side of a single ("Stand!" was on the flip), and its success this time around was supercharged by the song's strong placement in the Woodstock set. It sounded a rousing call for various means of enhanced experience. The Woodstock media quickly elevated the festival and several of its star acts, including Sly & the Family Stone, from the status of peak but flawed experiences to the status of myth. And the public is always hungry for myth, even when it obscures any clear-eyed view of what's really going down.

THE BIG MONEY SLY MADE after *Stand!* and its follow-ups helped him establish luxurious and well-protected bicoastal command points between 1969 and 1971, including an enviable suite on New York City's prestigious Central Park West. (As for the city of his early success, Sly was witnessed delivering a diatribe from the stage to a Bay Area audience in late '69. "You're over," he told the stunned crowd. "You thought you were cool, but your arrogance was your undoing, and San Francisco is now over, officially." "He didn't explain it," noted spectator Joel Selvin. "He was just pissed off.")

Down in Los Angeles, Stevie Swanigan was assigned responsibility of locating domiciles after Sly and David Kapralik had established an office for their new Stone Flower Productions in Hollywood. From an apartment in the Griffith Park area behind Hollywood, Sly moved to a larger, more removed rented property on Coldwater Canyon. Along with Topanga Canyon, Beverly Hills, and Bel Air, this was one of several select areas favored by L.A.'s rich and famous because they offered verdant hillsides, relative isolation, and spacious structures on large lots. Debbie King lived at the Coldwater Canyon property during that period of her connection with Sly, and Stevie and some of Sly's bandmates and acquaintances used it as a crash pad and base of operations, with a caretaker named Louis abiding on a more permanent basis. Joel Selvin, who made a visit to the property on behalf of his college paper, notes that "K. C. and Alpha [Stewart] were down at Coldwater Canyon a lot. They were somewhere between figurehead parents and kitchen staff." An expanding collection of dogs added to the visual and olfactory signs of life.

Hamp "Bubba" Banks, who'd provided Sly with rowdy company and something of a template of toughness on the streets of San Francisco, reconnected with Sly after spending some time in prison. He found his friend mutated by fame and fortune, and more desirous of services Bubba and some of his streetwise colleagues were quite ready to provide, including facilitating and protecting Sly's indulgences. "When I got to Los Angeles, he was the cocaine king," Bubba recalled. "Now he could really do what he wanted. . . . If I was in the house, he could do what he wanted." Joel reveals that Bubba was disappointed with K. C.'s relationship to Sly during this period, because "his son was irresponsible, disrespectful, a piece of shit, and K. C. let him be that way . . . 'cause the guy was cleaning toilets until his son had a hit record, and when they bought that place on Urbano Drive, Daddy didn't have to clean toilets no more. . . . So he'd put up with anything."

Bubba himself deserves some thanks, or blame, for letting Sly be himself, or what he'd become, a dynamo of both creativity for occasional public consumption and of extravagant private indulgence. The latter, of course, came to compromise the former. "He didn't have to ask for it, he didn't have to buy," Stephani Owens told Joel about the easy availability of substances for those with the right amount of cash and/or the right connections. "There were some drugs around that were bought, but not as much as were given to him. . . . Life was drugs, and it was music." While recording at the Record Plant, near San Francisco, "They would spend so many hours, thirty-six to forty-eight hours in a stretch, wearing out the engineers. But they were doing drugs too."

Freddie told Joel that PCP, aka angel dust, was introduced into the array of stimulants at his brother's L.A. digs as early as New Year's Eve 1969. PCP (phencyclidine hydrochloride) had been labeled a "dissociative anesthetic" and removed from its original use in human and veterinary medicine because of its threatening and unpredictable side effects, including psychotic reactions and a speculative link to permanent brain damage. But some of its effects, including a removal from bodily and environmental reality and a desensitizing of reactions to pain, had brought the drug back into recreational use.

Freddie recalled that on that drugged New Year's Eve, two PCP users had to be rushed to the hospital. Over the next year, Hamp "Bubba" Banks observed the effects of PCP on both of the Stewart/Stone brothers: "[Sly] and Freddie walked around the house all day, like zombies," he told Joel. "That is where it all fell apart."

Drug use and self-indulgent behavior were becoming common among successful musicians. Their lifestyles were substantially financed by advances paid to them against their future earnings, and recording companies were only too ready to provide the cash and to tolerate indications of excess. "The more popular you get," Sly pointed out to *Spin* magazine in 1985, "the more people there are around you who say they will make everything work. So more people make money off your hide, like from traveling arrangements. . . . When you're much younger and on top, they tell you, 'Don't worry 'bout nothin'. Hey, you're an artist, just worry about your music.' . . . I'd get a lot of contracts crammed in my face. I'd be getting into a Learjet, on my way somewhere, and they'd say, 'Before you get to the next place, can we see you, sweetheart? Sign this right quick.'" Along with the cash, it became ever easier for Sly to acquire roadies, personal assistants, and luxury vehicles. Ultimately, of course, it became more difficult for him to fulfill the terms of those contracts and to put aside any part of the money toward his financial future; most of it disappeared in the short run.

With a more hopeful approach to finances, Sly and David Kapralik's Stone Flower Productions was set up in an office opposite the distinctive cylindrical headquarters of Capitol Records in Hollywood. Drawing on the producing skills he'd first honed as a teenager at Autumn Records, Sly helped launch a brief but successful career (on Atlantic Records) for Little Sister, the group named for his youngest musical sibling, Vet. She was joined by two other vocalists, Mary McCreary and Elva "Tiny" Mouton, with whom she'd attended high school, performed gospel music (as the Heavenly Tones), and later provided backup on her older brother's albums. In 1970, Little Sister placed on the pop and R & B charts with two of Sly's compositions, "Somebody's Watching You" (a cover from the Family Stone's *Stand!* album) and "You're the One." Stone Flower also produced less successful recordings by R & B artist Joe Hicks and the proto-funk group 6iX. Notable in these productions was Sly's novel use of a prototype drum machine, a harbinger of developments in Sly's own later recordings and in popular music in general.

Sly made several carefully selected concert appearances across the country in 1970. One of those stops, for a free concert in Chicago's Grant Park on July 27, resulted in what was described in subsequent national reports and in legend for decades to come as "a riot."

As reported in the *New York Times*, "several thousand youths" battled police and vandalized the city's Loop district after the Family Stone refused to perform at the concert. Presented by the city as "a way to bridge the generation gap," the concert featured Sly as a form of apology to fans who'd been disappointed when he'd welched on dates earlier in the summer. The band, however, refused to begin playing for the free concert until the crowd quieted itself, which it didn't. The *Times* piece didn't lay blame on Sly for the Chicago riot, but other parts of the press and the rumor among the public nationwide did. It didn't help that Sly & the Family Stone were accumulating blame for showing up late for gigs or missing them altogether, trying the patience of young audiences. Besides, the health of rock concerts in general had become suspect, after the fatality and chaos of the Altamont Free Concert, featuring the Rolling Stones, in December 1969.

Epic's Al DeMarino is still eager to clear the record about the Chicago fiasco. "There was racial tension against the police force well before this day was scheduled," he claims. "In fact, bricks were found, chains were found, bats were found, prior to the band coming out. So they didn't cause it by not performing, it was caused by tension before. . . . And Irv Kupcinet, a great writer in Chicago [for the *Sun-Times*], was the only one who came forth days later and said, listen, this has nothing to do with Sly & the Family Stone. . . . I gave a radio interview to Gene Loving, a major disc jockey . . . and explained everything to him, because he cared enough and wanted to know the truth. And I referred to Irv Kupcinet's column."

Later that summer, Sly left the accusations (but not his self-indulgent habits) behind and made an extensive sweep through Western Europe, including a stop at the Olympia, Paris's oldest music hall (where he would stage a comeback, with Vet, thirty-seven summers later). The expatriated Ria Boldway was alerted to

Sly's visit and got to experience him in a context very different from the hometown boy she'd hung with; Sly was now an ascending international celebrity.

Ria had moved to Paris in 1968 to study at the American College, learn French, and start a performing career. Attractive, talented, and quickly bilingual, she landed a role in the French-language production of *Hair: The Tribal-Rock Love Musical*, which had been luring younger audiences to Broadway with its pop-oriented score and episode of onstage nudity. For a long time, Ria kept herself deliberately ignorant of the Family Stone's path to fame and fortune: "I didn't buy any of his stuff." Even now, "I've still never read any books written about him, because I thought it would hurt way too much," she says. But back in Paris, "I remember one day going over to my friend Paul's flat, we were all going to study music for this anthropology course. And Paul said, 'I got this new album, let's put it on.' And I almost died! It was *Dance to the Music*. . . . I thought it was wonderful."

Ria thus came to Sly bearing kudos, but she noted that after she told him about being featured in *Hair*, there was no complimentary reciprocation. "You know, what really hurt was he never said he was proud of me for being in the most successful play in Paris, which was comparable to being on the New York stage for three and a half years. He just didn't acknowledge it. . . . The whole [Family Stone] band was invited to come and see our show, we gave them tickets and treated them like royalty. I was given [a variety of roles] to perform that night, specially for my friends. And he didn't come."

The disappointed Ria had to admit to herself how far Sly had wandered along the metaphorical road she'd seen him moving down four years earlier, in the white convertible with Carol Doda.

Still, the old flames spent much time together during Sly's week in the City of Light. "He was fairly unreachable, as far as depth of emotion and real contact went," she reports. "He was that way with everybody. . . . As far as I could tell, he didn't have private conversations with anybody anymore. He didn't hang out with the group, stayed by himself, pretty much a different person." The rest of the Family Stone, in turn, "was looking down in the mouth, the whole band." Nevertheless, despite a now-familiar hour's delay in starting, Sly and the ensemble were able to mount "a damn good show" at the Olympia, with Ria cheering from the audience. "The staging was beautiful, the costuming was excellent," she says. "Very much the whole *Hair* thing, the whole hippie movement thing. And the vocals were excellent."

Looking back on the after-show activities at Sly's hotel, Ria realizes how naïve she was then about the chemical influences on his behavior. "Sly said, 'Hey, Ria, can you get me some coke?' And I said, 'Man, it's kind of late, but I'll try.' I called up the frigging concierge and was trying for about an hour to order *Coca-Cola* at around two in the morning. . . . He'd always told me I was lame, and I guess he was right." During that week, Ria noticed that Sly "would spend so much time in the bathroom with different people. Not girls, guys. They'd go in there, and I had no idea what it was about."

There was a parting of the ways when Sly moved on to tour dates in Holland. He returned to the States, to deal with the volatile mix of celebrity and infamy that he and the press had been stirring up. Ria herself crossed back over the Atlantic two years later, with a husband (who wanted her to give up show biz) and their two children. Another reunion with Sly awaited, further down his hard road.

Riot

— 1970–1972 —

No one understands another's grief, no one understands another's joy. . . . My music is the product of my talent and my misery. And that which I have written in my greatest distress is what the world seems to like the best.

—FRANZ SCHUBERT

Man seeks to escape himself in myth, and does so by any means at his disposal. Drugs, alcohol, or lies. Unable to withdraw into himself, he disguises himself.

—JEAN COCTEAU

WHILE WAITING OUT THE two years for a new album after *Stand!*, Columbia gave fans a recap of what they'd already learned to love about Sly & the Family Stone. *Greatest Hits*, the band's first compilation, was released in 1970, and its tracks were almost consistently positive and uplifting.

On ABC-TV's *The Dick Cavett Show* in July 1970, though, the band presented a different image to its fans, less the Summer of

Love fantasy of the past than the tough streetwise attitude that would become associated with their next album, *There's a Riot Goin' On*. Sly and Cynthia had expanded their hairstyles to sizeable Afros, Jerry and Greg's hair had lengthened, Rose was tough and beautiful, and Freddie was topped by a swami's turban. After a tight performance of their new single, "Thank You (Falettinme Be Mice Elf Agin)," Sly ambled over to the guest area for a loose quasi-conversation with the host. Sly made for a curious visual and aural contrast with Dick and his other guest, the chipper '50s star Debbie Reynolds.

"Could I dress like this and play in your group?" the buttoned-down Cavett needled Sly. "Wouldn't it look funny?"

"With people that were judging the way you were dressing," Sly responded dully in a low-register mumble.

"There'd probably be a certain pressure on me . . ." speculated Cavett.

"There's a pressure on all of us," said Sly truthfully. How much of Sly's demeanor in a number of TV appearances was due to pre-show drugging (to which there were witnesses) and how much to his lifelong fondness for shuck and jive is speculative, as is his impact on TV viewers, who themselves varied in age and hipness and reaction to the image of a charismatic and seemingly uncontrollable black man.

"Thank You (Falettinme Be Mice Elf Agin)" had been released as a single in December 1969 and became one of the biggest hits of 1970, scoring a number 1 spot on both the pop and R & B lists. Riding on a seismic, octave-jumping bass line from Larry and punctuated with Freddie's choked treble chords, the music dug an irresistible groove, matched by the lyric's clever name-checks of some of the band's previous tunes: "Dance to the Music," "Sing a Simple Song," "You Can Make It If You Try," and "Everyday People." Just as the groove was a sign of the funk to come, the quirky parenthetical title anticipated Prince, who would make phonetic spelling one of his signature riffs, as would hip-hop stars of later decades. "Thank You" was a double-A release, with the radiant and very different "Everybody Is a Star"—on which all the Family vocalists, Sly, Larry, Cynthia, Freddie, and Rose—individually shared one of Sly's most positive lyrics and the band's most loving arrangements, evoking the good vibes that were in practice starting to slip away from their lives and music. (These two songs, along with "Hot Fun in the Summertime," were the only non-album tracks on *Greatest Hits*.)

You can hear in "Thank You" and "Everybody Is a Star" the sound that would influence a number of brassy rock ensembles throughout the '70s and later. There would be currents of the Family's spiritualized, horn-honking soul and funk in bands like Blood, Sweat & Tears; Chicago; in spurts in the Rolling Stones; and more distantly in Santana and Steely Dan.

The popular judgment on *Riot* is that it's evidence of Sly's fall from a state of sunlit grace into a miasma of dark introspection, fueled by chemical self-indulgence. In the wider cultural context, the album is pictured as an accompaniment to the Baby Boomers' disillusioned rejection of idealism, based on the preceding years' scourge of assassinations, war, political intrigue, and bad drugs.

Riot does in fact sound different from much of what preceded it, and in looking more closely at Sly's personal circumstances during the production of the album, likely influences on its sound can be discovered. Making too tight a tie between that sound and social and historical circumstances is tempting but fallacious, since much of what was happening to the world in 1971, as well as some of what was happening in Sly's life, had in fact already been happening in the years when Sly and the band were putting out rather different kinds of albums, and would continue for some while after. But 1971, the year of *Riot*, is a good point from which to take a look at the times, however little Sly himself may have been prone to such reflection.

Attention among Americans in the '70s was shifted toward more militant manifestations of black pride. The civil rights movement, focused on righting wrongs perpetrated by whites on blacks, had resulted in the federally enforced Civil Rights Act of 1964, with marches and protests before and after. The assassination of Martin Luther King Jr., in 1968, was a shock to all Americans, but it didn't do away with peaceful protest. The most visible of the militant groups, the Black Panther Party, had been founded back in 1966 in Oakland, while Sly was still gigging in North Beach on the other side of the San Francisco Bay. By the time of *Riot*, the Black Panthers' power and presence in the press had grown alongside Sly's, and it was no surprise that party members started making overtures to Sly, Jimi Hendrix, and other reigning black rockers. But Sly clearly wasn't interested. His action in assembling a racially and gender-integrated unit spoke louder than any of his rare public declarations on racism, and the Family Stone, unlike some rock and folk acts, never manifested itself as part of civil rights demonstrations or the movement overall. Instead, the band expressed its collective consciousness on the subject in musical form, most famously in "Everyday People," "Underdog," and most explicitly "Don't Call Me Nigger, Whitey."

Critic Greil Marcus, in his 1974 book *Mystery Train*, noted, "With this album [*Riot*], Sly is giving his audience—particularly his white audience—precisely what they don't want. What they want from Sly is an upper, not a portrait of what lies behind his big freaky black superstar grin. One gets the feeling, listening to this album, that Sly's disastrous concerts of the past year have not been so much a matter of insulting his audience as attacking it, with real bitterness and hate, because of what its demands on him have forced him to produce. It is an attack on himself as well, for having gone along with those demands."

The shooting of students at Kent State in 1970 shocked but failed to stop those who'd been protesting the Vietnam War on U.S. college campuses since the early '60s. By 1969, wider protests were moving tens of thousands of people of all ages along the streets of San Francisco and other cities. Among the growing number of bands collectively referred to as being part of the San Francisco sound were several with antiwar messages in their lyrics, most notably Country Joe and the Fish and the Jefferson Airplane. These and other acts, along with folk performers like Bob Dylan, Joan Baez, and Pete Seeger, provided inspiration at larger gatherings for peace. Creedence Clearwater Revival (which started in El Cerrito, a few minutes south of Vallejo) got their wailing rocker of a protest song, "Fortunate Son," onto the charts in the autumn of 1969. Other successful antiwar tunes included John Lennon's "Give Peace a Chance," in '69, Jimi Hendrix's "Machine Gun," and Crosby, Stills, Nash, and Young's "Ohio," both in '70. From the sector of soul and R & B, there were Edwin Starr's "War" and the Temptations' "Ball of Confusion (That's What the World Is Today)," also in '70, and Marvin Gaye's "What's Going On" the next year. Sly & the Family Stone sang even less about war than they did about racism, though their apparent promotion of life and self-realization allowed them to keep company with artists making clearer statements of resistance.

Allusions to drugs, marijuana in particular, can be discovered in the lyrics of some of the songs on Bob Dylan's *Blonde on Blonde*, Jimi Hendrix's *Are You Experienced*, and the Beatles' *Sgt. Pepper's*

Lonely Hearts Club Band. Drugs aren't specifically referenced in any of Sly & the Family Stone's lyrics, although they certainly figured in the band's creative process long before the making of *Riot*, and over-indulgence in harder drugs affected the production of that and later albums.

"We were a pot-smoking, wine-drinking band until cocaine was introduced," Jerry Martini pointed out to Joel Selvin. This change of habits was not to be taken lightly. Marijuana, relatively inexpensive and available, might be said to have furthered some of the ideals promoted in Sly's earlier lyrics, including the relaxation of differences, the pursuit of happiness, and the enjoyment of social and personal love. For Sly's and the Baby Boomers generation, powders and pills generally came along later and at a greater cost, literally and figuratively.

Cocaine and amphetamines could also function as a means toward the end of sustaining high energy and production. None of this, of course, could guarantee a great musical experience. The celebrity and money, which peaked for the Family Stone after Woodstock, meant that the band members could attract sources of cocaine and afford to maintain serial highs, as well as to obtain prescription drugs. Jerry told Joel that the band at one point had in tow a physician who "was really impressed with the music business [and] felt that Sly needed . . . psychosedatives. . . . You wake up, take Placidyl, which [Sly] got from his doctor. Then, you snort enough cocaine until you can talk straight. It was like this up-and-down roller coaster." There were reports that at some point, Sly may have had cocaine prescribed for relief from an ulcer. Stephani Owens told Joel Selvin how, during her early days of service as a personal assistant to Sly, he'd shared some pharmaceutical cocaine with her. "As it turns out, he was getting his drugs from the dentist," she said. "Then I found out there was a doctor in New York that would give him and anybody in the group prescription drugs, yellow jackets [downers], et cetera."

Sly seemed to be finding it difficult to get off the roller coaster in time to make it to his bookings, nearby and on tour. "He used to cancel, which also used to piss me off," Jerry related for Joel. "He would have six months of fantastic bookings, then, at the last minute, he would cancel them. He was incapable of going on the road, as he had for the last twenty years. Incapable of functioning as a traveling musician, doing what he could do so well." "He was never on time," said Stephani in *Mojo* magazine. "It was always an effort to get the band to the gig and get them onstage on time. . . . It was mostly Freddie and Sly because even when the rest of the group would catch a commercial flight and do what they were supposed to do, with Freddie and Sly, I would be trying to find a private plane for them to go on." Sly gave his own explanation later to *Vanity Fair* about his perennial tardiness for gigs, suggesting that promoters and roadies encouraged this behavior so that they could profit from it: "I got tired of going to concerts where I'd have to pay a bond, pay money in case I didn't show up," he admitted. "I later found out that they had a deal going between the promoter and the guy that was taking me to the gig. So I would put up the $25,000 or the $50,000. The guy with me would help me be late, and I didn't realize that was what was going on until later. Then they'd split the money. . . . I wasn't so focused after a while." Whatever the setup, Sly was five hours late for a show in Washington, D.C., causing a fan melee outside the venue of Constitution Hall in early 1970. He ducked out of five concerts in succession a year later, his excuse, quoted in *Rolling Stone*, being simply, "Sometimes you don't feel your soul at seven-thirty."

There was a long wait also for Sly and the band's next recorded product, and CBS officials were getting a little nervous. "I'd be fibbing if I said I wasn't somewhat concerned," says Epic's Al DeMarino, "but [Sly's] back catalog was selling constantly, and there was promoter interest and press interest. I had great confidence that he could do it." David Kapralik's confidence was waning. "I had no influence on what Sly was doing," he told *Mojo*. "I was managing the unmanageable. . . . His two personas—the shy, innocent poet Sylvester Stewart and the streetwise character he'd invented, Sly Stone—were torn apart. He numbed himself with cocaine." Clive Davis, who headed Epic, was of two minds. "At some point, I started getting concerned about stories I heard about Sly's personal habits," he recalled for *Vanity Fair*. "But every time I met with him, he was on top of his game. I was somewhat innocent of the lifestyle going on around me, whether it was him or Janis Joplin."

For those fans financially able to partake of pills and powders, harder drugs might provide the illusion of sharing, at least for a while, the high life of performers. Whatever uppers or downers may have been shared by the fans at Madison Square Garden in September 1971, the effect was not lost on Don Heckman, reviewing for *The New York Times*. "The sheer, exuberant joy that I've seen flowing out of the audiences at Sly's past concerts seems to have been replaced by an almost desperate self-conditioning," he wrote, "a sheer determination that dancing up and down, singing 'higher, higher, higher,' waving, whistling, and shouting will somehow revive the old magic. But it isn't working, because the Family Stone sounds as though it is just going through the motions. . . . Could it be that the milk and honey have been flowing too freely in the gardens of the gods?"

There's a Riot Goin' On took form not in any godly garden, but in the Record Plant, a new state-of-the-art recording studio in Northern California, and at what Jerry Martini described as "a stately mansion," at 783 Bel Air Road, near Beverly Hills. Formerly the home of '30s screen sweetheart Jeannette MacDonald, it bore evidence of its more recent occupants, John and Michelle Phillips, of the Mamas and Papas, a '60s folk-rock group. There was a home recording studio, installed by John Phillips, a small buffet of drugs, and a general mess. Sly had connected with the property, which he rented for a reputed $12,000 a month, through Terry Melcher, who was the son of Doris Day and a well-connected party animal favored by the young entertainers of the late '60s and early '70s, among them John and Michelle, the Beach Boys' Dennis Wilson, and actress Candice Bergen. Terry had established success as producer of his mother's television show and of records for Columbia, but he also embodied the spendthrift wealth and casual debauchery of young Hollywood. Dennis Wilson had introduced Terry to ex-convict and would-be mass murderer Charles Manson, in hopes of furthering the latter's songwriting aspirations.

Recording at 783 Bel Air Road commenced in the autumn of 1970. The resulting music lacked the live, spacious ambience of the whole band playing together in real time, so much a part of the appeal of earlier albums. Instead, the tracks that would be used on *Riot* favored a compressed, claustrophobic density, in part due to endless overdubs that actually threatened to wear out the magnetic oxide coating on the recording tape. Sly Stone annotator Alec Palao shares a report about this process, which is corroborated in part by Jerry Martini. "Sly would pick these girls up at L.A. clubs and say, 'Baby, I want you to sing on my record.' They'd be high on cocaine, he'd record them at two in the morning, warbling along, and then the next morning he'd wipe the tape" and dismiss the musical and romantic one-nighter. In any case, the fidelity on the album is unusual and somehow intimate; listen to the breathy wetness and directness of Sly's voice on "Family Affair."

Outside John Phillips' studio, Sly did much taping in a Winnebago camper parked near the mansion and fitted with state-of-the-art recording gear. The original Family Stone members were in and out, logging tracks individually, and holding on to Sly for a variety of reasons, among them the supply of cocaine.

But Larry, Greg, and Freddie started spending more time in Northern California, and Sly was supplying more of his own bass and guitar parts, also supplementing his rhythm needs with a drum machine. Greg credits the album with extending Sly's talent and vision. "He was one of the first to take the drum machine and make it be an instrument," concedes the flesh-and-blood drummer. "The machine, as opposed to what it is now [i.e., high-tech computerized programs], was a lounge instrument that the guy at the bar at the Holiday Inn might have used. Sly took the ticky-tacky, which started on the 'tick,' and he inverted it, turned it inside out, into something the ear wasn't used to. He took the texture and created a rhythm with it that made it very interesting." From the man-versus-machine perspective, "I don't think the trade-off was good," Greg insists, but he points out that Sly had become attracted to synthesized percussion well before its use on *Riot*.

While the band's bonds of togetherness frayed, Sly kept company with Bubba Banks (who at this point was married to Rose) and James "J. B." Brown (Bubba's buddy, not the Godfather of Soul), and he received visits from musicians Ike Turner, Bobby Womack, jazz legend and enfant terrible Miles Davis, and Sly's old friend Billy Preston, who'd gone on to play with everyone from Ray Charles to the Beatles. It can be assumed that any or all of these visitors shared recorded jams, inspired by snorts of coke. Billy provided the artful keyboards on "Family Affair," and Bobby and Miles may be somewhere in the mix, but it's likely that nobody had a chance to get very comfortable.

"I was always thinking I was gonna get killed and that the feds were gonna bust in on Sly," Bobby told *Vanity Fair*. "Everybody had pistols . . . Sly be talkin' to you, but he ain't there. He'd be lying on the piano whacked out of his brain when it was time to do a vocal, and they'd have to lay the microphone next to his head." For his autobiography, Miles Davis recollected, "I went to a couple [of recording sessions] and there were nothing but girls everywhere and coke, bodyguards with guns, looking all evil. I told him I couldn't do nothing with him—told Columbia I couldn't make him record any quicker. We snorted some coke together and that was it."

Jerry, although he'd return to Sly periodically to help burnish recording projects, described to Joel Selvin how he extricated himself from the drug-driven L.A. residence. "I got in my jeep, put my dog and my wife in, and went back up to my house [in Marin County, across the Golden Gate Bridge from San Francisco]. Left no notice, and didn't talk to [Sly] for a couple of months." Greg was the soonest to escape from an orbit around Sly altogether, returning to his own Marin home. He noted to Joel that, after his departure, "I'd get daily calls from [Sly], from everybody, and I just didn't want no more part of it. It wasn't fun anymore. . . . The business was handled very poorly. . . . I had seen the situation deteriorate and seen [Sly] not responding to it, refusing to respond to the needs of everybody on all different levels. It got ugly within the group, around the group, the audience, the whole thing. . . . Then I made a decision, emotionally: I cut the umbilical cord." *Riot* was the last album with Greg named as a member of the Family Stone. On some cuts, Sly augmented the drum machine with his own live beats on hi-hat cymbals, creating a complex mélange of the real and the robotic, and a brand-new rhythm sound that would continue to captivate listeners.

On *Riot*'s biggest hit, "Family Affair," the Rhythm Ace, an ancestor of the synthesizers and sequencers that power contemporary urban music, thrummed electronically under Rose's choruses, Billy Preston's keyboards, Freddie's ghetto guitar, and Sly's seductively languid vocal. Stephen Paley, at that point working for CBS's Clive Davis, notes that his boss was skeptical about "Family Affair" before its release as a single. "[Clive] said, 'That sounds like he's stoned. We can't put that out.' And I said, 'Clive, it's okay, it won't matter, it's a great record.'"

It was, and so were most of the album's diverse other tracks. "Africa Talks to You 'The Asphalt Jungle'" was a long, loose jam, and "(You Caught Me) Smilin'" had some of the same shag-carpet sexy feel of "Family Affair." *Riot* also revels in solid soul on "Time," and in a very different and capricious mode, a yodeling tribute to Sly's childhood idols on "Spaced Cowboy." "Thank You for Talkin' to Me Africa" was a slinky, slowed-down retake of "Thank You (Falletinme Be Mice Elf Agin)." As for the title track, with its noted "0:00" timing (there are no sounds), Sly told Jon Dakss in 1997, "I did it because I felt there should be no riots."

Riot was finally released in November 1971, with a cover that depicted an altered American flag, with suns instead of stars, hanging above the fireplace at 783 Bel Air Road. Also on the cover was a composite photo collage of persons involved with the album and other aspects of Sly's life. But it was the first Family cover with no band members depicted. In a year that also heard the debuts of Marvin Gaye's *What's Going On*, the Who's *Who's Next*, the Rolling Stones' *Sticky Fingers*, and Led Zeppelin's *Led Zeppelin IV*, *Riot* proved as easy for the public to be motivated to purchase, in large amounts, as it was difficult for them to comprehend and categorize. Reviewers, however, seemed quick to project onto the album their own alarm about changing times and a changing Sly, vacillating between criticism and praise for his new modes of expression.

"The album is a testament to two years of deterioration rather than two years of growth," wrote Vince Aletti in *Rolling Stone*, before allowing, "Once you get into the haze of it, it can be rather beautiful: measured, relaxed, hypnotic." Greil Marcus reviewed the album three times for *Creem*, admitting that "we're confused by it." He compared *Riot* to "Van Morrison's *Blowin' Your Mind*, his first solo album, where Van reached for the grotesque because it seemed the only adequate description of everyday life; Dylan's *John Wesley Harding*, in that Sly is escaping his own past; and Lennon's *Plastic Ono Band*, though Sly is working with much greater sophistication and control." Less concerned with postulating indicators of personal and general decline, Greil insisted, "The success of this new album is that it is simultaneously deeply personal and inescapably political, innovative and tough in its music, literate and direct in its words, a parody of the past and a strong and unflinching statement about the present."

Suggestive of the power and influence of the entire album is the degree to which the deep, brooding funk of tracks like "Luv N' Haight" and "Brave and Strong" earned homage on Stevie Wonder's work later in the '70s, particularly *Innervisions* (1973) and *Songs in the Key of Life* (1976). Sly's keyboard on the "Poet" track is a particularly clear antecedent to "Just Enough for the City" by Stevie, whose social commentary was more explicit than Sly's, though in a similar somber mode. Throughout Stevie's lyrics, there were echoes of Sly's fanciful tricking out of the English language, an aspect of poetic prowess rarely encountered in rock or any other song form. Sly's and Stevie's more serious approach to songwriting was shared by writer-musician Gil Scott-Heron, who fused politically charged verses with a kind of jazz-funk accompaniment

("The Bottle," "The Revolution Will Not Be Televised"). And Marvin Gaye was getting more serious, moving from his charming origins in Motown hits to the powerfully honest "What's Going On" and the bedroom confessional of 1973's "Let's Get It On."

Apart from the myths about its creation and critical commentary on its content, it's entirely possible, and certainly advisable, to appreciate *Riot* for its good tracks, not necessarily better or worse than any other part of Sly's output, and for its imagination and spirit, as well as for its significant, if not singular, place in the evolution of Sly's music and popular music in general. Also memorable are the artful lyrics, presenting an unglossy examination of personal relationships, rare in rock. ("Family Affair," often judged as melancholy, actually showcases scenes of positive family values alongside those of interpersonal insecurity.) It's important to realize that *Riot* didn't signal a complete or permanent darkening of Sly's expression. Despite his continuing dependence on drugs over the next decade, several of the albums recorded by Sly during that period exhibit considerable brightness, both musically and lyrically

In a recent interview for this book, Sly himself talks about an influence on the album unfamiliar to most, from within the record business. "People were coming from all different kinds of record companies," he points out. "People were talking to different people in the group, and telling me that I didn't need this person or that person, or telling [the group's members] how they didn't need this or that person. They break you up so they can have different concerts every night, and make everybody different stars, with different record sales. Those record companies have people (and I won't say their names right now) whose job was to infiltrate inside an organized musical endeavor and separate and divide it up." Sly says he tried to warn his colleagues about this purported threat, but they "really weren't seeing it. They were like, 'They don't really mean that, do they?' and I was, 'Yeah, that's what they mean.'" He hopes that reflective fans will "put things together and notice that, 'Oh yeah, when that record was out, that's when they got separated, and that's when that argument started.'"

Sly couldn't deny, though, that the breakup of the band, however encouraged by outside forces, was also seriously exacerbated by misuse of drugs. He may have been controlling the distribution of cocaine to those around him, but that kind of activity inevitably spins out of control. The strain of induced ups and downs on Bel Air Road simultaneously prompted both Sly's self-centered approach to music making and his band members' alienation from him. And drugs deteriorated Sly's sense of professional and financial responsibility.

Al DeMarino has his own take on Sly becoming more dependent on substances during this phase: "Between the pressure of stardom, family pressure, social pressures, cultural pressures, and a habit that was becoming consuming, it made for a difficult moment in time." Al and some others at Columbia and Epic attempted interventions with Sly. "There were discussions with him, and eventually he tried rehab programs. Perhaps it would have been better for all of us, starting with him, if he had started sooner. [Drugs] altered his personality upon occasion. Those who loved him dearly were hurt, because it changed him in a certain way. He wasn't as positive and as open and warm as he had once been. . . . It would hurt me. . . . I would talk to him, others would talk to him—as opposed to the hangers-on, who were always looking to get some free blow—and I would say, 'Sylvester, what are we doing here?' And he'd respond, 'I know you love me, and I'm in control.' Famous last words."

In conversation with Joel Selvin, Bubba Banks testified how he had functioned as the "pit bull that lived good" at Sly's residences, while Sly, as "the controller," determined who got how much of which drugs when. "Nobody had their own blow, he was the man, and that is where he gets his audience." The audience at times included band members, numbed into a very different relationship with the band's leader. They included brother Freddie, who managed to make occasional trips to his own home in the Oakland Hills to dry out.

Jerry marks the move to Los Angeles as the inception of the troubles. Sly amassed a collection of vicious dogs, intimidating most visitors and temporary residents. Frank Arellano, working to establish himself as a musician in L.A. and living a safer life, was invited to Bel Air several times on the strength of his credentials as a singer with Sly in the Viscaynes. He found that his former schoolmate and singing partner "wasn't the same guy. He wasn't as relaxed and loose, he was more rigid and seemed serious." While Sly's father was still functioning as the band's road manager, K. C. Stewart had seemed to turn a blind eye to his son's use of drugs, and after he'd retired from those duties and returned to San Francisco, the one- time warm and regular contact between Sly and his parents became undependable.

"I think cocaine is one of the largest industry-dismantling vehicles," says Jerry. "The downfall of the most famous bands was largely due to the affiliates, the hangers-on, the dealers, the doctors. . . . [With] everybody we were on tour with, it happened to most of the other bands back then. I don't want to talk about other bands and stuff that I saw, though. . . . It's kind of a scary thing, and it leaves me open to a lot of criticism." During the late '60s and throughout the '70s, the world of rock was indeed populated by many with addictions of various durations to various drugs. The usual suspects included Elton John, Eric Clapton, Marvin Gaye, Billy Preston,

James Taylor, James Brown, David Bowie, and some within the Beatles, the Rolling Stones, the Who, Led Zeppelin, the Grateful Dead, the Temptations, the Allman Brothers, and Aerosmith.

Following Sly to his den on the West Coast, manager David Kapralik was among those lining up for white lines. But the drug couldn't fill in the widening cracks in David's idealized picture of Sly as a paradigm of progressive social consciousness and in his view of himself as an able, anointed caretaker. Kitsaun King, the older sister of Sly's former girlfriend Debbie King and herself a one-time employee of Stone Flower Productions, commented to Joel on the saddening role David played out at Sly's L.A. homesteads in the early 1970s. "You expected people like the David Kapraliks, the people who were adults, who had been in the music business, and who, in theory, had some knowledge, to be telling Sly the truth. But they weren't telling the truth. They were just going along with Sly's program. And Sly's program was totally substandard, because he was high all the time."

David recalls, "this whole *mise-en-scène* in this dank, dank house in Bel Air. Various characters were walking around with guns. And there was Gunn the dog, the terrifier. It was heavy. Let's just leave it at that. And I didn't want to live anymore." The formerly confident and buoyant David felt profoundly shaken by what he perceived as the dissolution of his relationship with Sly, who had been under pressure from his older sister Loretta Stewart and from the Black Panthers to "get rid of whitey." Ultimately, after the release of *Riot*, David "went on my knees before [Sly] to let me bring in Ken Roberts to manage him, so that I could go on and live." David was well aware of Ken's reputation, still in place today, for cool-headed, bottom-line management of talent and other enterprises.

Having done his best to attend to Sly's future, David decided to shorten his own. He describes the scenario. "One day, I forget what I was on, I was on the whole alphabet at the time, I called a taxicab to take me to the Beverly Hills Hotel. I took two bags, so I could check in. Threw clothes into them. . . . I'd been going to the Beverly Hills Hotel for years. So there I was at the desk, wavering more than a little bit . . . 'Good afternoon, Mr. Kapralik!' [said the bell captain], and then, to the bellman, 'Bungalow A'. Now, Bungalow A was where Richard Burton and Elizabeth Taylor had their first honeymoon. And it's a scene, in pink satin and gilt, everywhere, in the furniture, in the ceilings. And that's all I had on me: guilt, guilt, guilt, for all that had and hadn't happened in my life."

Why did David blame himself for what he'd perceived as an unanticipated spoiling of his plans for Sly? It was "the thought that before Sylvester's eyes I had dissembled, disintegrated, fallen apart emotionally . . . and [it was] exacerbated by seeing this image, this vision, this expression of my heart-song to the world [that is, Sly] crumbling before me.

"So I tipped the bellman, was all alone in the bungalow, which had a big, big living room and a big, big bedroom. And I was sitting at this ivory and gilt desk, writing a suicide note, and taking a fistful of Nembutal. . . . I was in a lot of pain. And suddenly I say to myself, 'I'm hungry.' So I reach for the telephone. I'd been there numerous times in the past, so I could do this with my gut overflowing with the Nembutal, beginning to take its effect. 'Mr. Kapralik in Bungalow A, service for one.' Final exit time, right? Would you like to know the menu of my last supper? Nova Scotia lox, bagels, whitefish, Bella Sol Beluga caviar, with quail eggs. And then champagne, Neuf de Chandon 1952. Of course, that's every Jew's comfort food I'd just ordered. And I think it was my mother's voice I heard from beyond: 'Don't forget your buttermilk!' I'd always loved buttermilk. But let me tell you, it saved my life. Because, the food came, I ate it, champagne and all, with a ritual toast for the big exit, right? And I took the glass of buttermilk and went into the bedroom to expire. Then, the buttermilk curdled in my stomach, with the lox and the whitefish and the new pickles. I ended up at the UCLA emergency ward, they're pumping my stomach, bringing me back to life, and I'm cursing the doctors and Sylvester Stewart/Sly Stone."

After David had returned to responsibility in his life, including the financial, he found himself facing a fee of five thousand bucks for clean-up of the bungalow bedroom's Persian rug. Not long after, he abandoned show biz to raise onions and flowers on the island of Maui. He left plenty of people on the mainland who were ready to share, and further, his former client's obsessions, but few who could reach David's level of fervent inspired devotion. Sly, though he'd come under the watch of Ken Roberts, continued to wear a Star of David necklace (visible in photos) in tribute to the man who helped launch his career.

The challenges of traveling alongside Sly in the coke-powered fast lane separated out those companions who wanted to help him get back on the right track from those who wanted to speed along beside him, scoring pieces of him in the process. One of his most famous partners in infamy was jazz trumpet titan Miles Davis. More than for his imprint on Stevie Wonder, Sly gained credit beyond his own work for his musical impact on Miles, particularly as evidenced on *Bitches Brew*, recorded in 1969 and '70 for Columbia. The album infused elements of rhythmic funk and electrified instrumentation, and was seen as heralding the jazz-rock amalgamation that came to be called "fusion," a breakthrough in the ears of many younger jazz fans and a bane in the estimation of others. In time other jazz-rock stylists adapted the hybrid textures to popular acclaim: Weather Report, Return to Forever, and Herbie Hancock, who'd dropped in at the *Riot* house and whose 1973 album, *Headhunters*, featured a track called "Sly."

Miles had earlier been curious about Jimi Hendrix's musical inventiveness and commercial success, and had heard Sly wow the crowd at the '69 Newport Jazz Festival. But he was more fully exposed to the seductive sounds of the Family Stone and to Jimi's Experience by his girlfriend and short-term wife, Betty (Mabry) Davis, an ex-model and aspiring singer and songwriter many years his junior. "When I first heard Sly, I almost wore out those first two or three records," Miles testified in his biography, before turning critical and being mistaken about Sly's past: "Then he wrote a couple of other great things, and then he didn't write nothing because the coke had fucked him up and he wasn't a trained musician."

Betty Davis recalls having met Sly in the Bay Area before she'd met Miles and before she went on, after their marriage, to record three legendary albums of funk herself, the first produced by Greg Errico, who, along with Larry Graham, was also featured in her band. "I was at the Record Plant [in Sausalito] and they were having a party there, and [Sly] was at the party," says Betty. She "thought he was really great," musically, but found him, as many did, "a bit aloof" in person. Not so aloof, though, that he didn't try to hustle the long-limbed Betty, perhaps providing inspiration for the most popular track off her Errico-produced album, "If I'm in Luck I Might Get Picked Up." Later, "I turned Miles on to [Sly]," Betty verifies, "because I used to play him in the house all the time. 'Dance to the Music,' 'Family Affair' . . . [Miles] liked it, or else he would have told me to turn it off." Betty sings an admiring shout-out to Sly in the lyrics of "F.U.N.K." on her fabulous *Nasty Gal* album (1975).

Miles had been one of several regular celebrity visitors to Sly's Central Park West digs in New York City for several years by the time Ria Boldway made another loving appearance, in 1973. She'd just returned to California from Paris and had ended up consulting a psychiatrist about what she thought was culture shock. "He said, 'It sounds to me like you need to leave your husband,'" she laughs. "And I did. I had been planning to. And that's when I got back in touch with Sly. I guess I called his mother's house and left my phone number. I said, 'If he ever needs me, if there's ever trouble or anything, let him call me.'" Sly himself soon called her, "And he said, 'I need you to come to New York with me.'" Having hopped a plane to San Francisco, Sly drove over to Ria's and took her to his parents' house. Taking Ria aside, "They begged me to help him," she says. "They didn't out and out say what the problems were, they just said, 'He's having a lot of problems and we're worried about his health, and maybe he'll listen to you.'"

With time to gather only a few of her things, Ria flew with Sly back to New York, no doubt recalling their first plane trip together a dozen years earlier. After landing, "We stayed by ourselves for a couple of days, and it was absolutely wonderful," sighs Ria. "Then I stayed there for three months. But he was so heavily into his downward spiral then that there was just no hope." It was a period of high living, in more than one sense. "Very posh, little things everywhere, bodyguards everywhere." Since she'd come across the country with little luggage, and she and Sly were about the same, trim size, Ria took to wearing some of "his gorgeous leather clothes." Sly then financed her shopping trips to the ritzy pharmacy on the building's first floor, for cosmetics, and to Greenwich Village, for clothing. He topped off his gifts with a floor-length mink coat. "I used to go walking in Central Park," Ria says, "with a bodyguard and a mink coat. Can you believe it?"

Bubba Banks, still Sly's right-hand man, acted as guide for her shopping trips and as much more than just a bodyguard to Sly, says Ria. "Bubba was more like a valet . . . or, he could have been a very dear friend tending to a very sick buddy. . . . He would take [Sly] in and out of the bathtub, when he couldn't do it himself, and try to get him ready and on his feet for meetings at Columbia, and interviews." The "sickness," of course, was self-induced, and this time, unlike in Paris, Ria was aware of Sly's habits. "He did so many drugs [including PCP] that I thought, a few times, he would die. And Bubba had to take care of him. Many times." Bubba himself "may have tippled," Ria supposes, "but nobody used like Sly, poor baby." Whatever Bubba's reputation among others of Sly's associates, Ria "didn't ever see him implement anything bad. . . . He never said anything untoward, he never cursed, the 'f' word was never spoken."

The visiting Miles Davis left a cruder but laughable impression on Ria. "Miles was a real crazy asshole, if you ask me," she opines. "Extremely talented, but with a very bad personality. He'd be up to his elbows and eyebrows in cocaine, and sit by himself in the dark in one of the rooms most of the time." Sly's reigning bassist, Rustee Allen, served as an additional witness to the jazz giant's shenanigans. Rustee recalled to Joel Selvin when Miles "got on Sly's organ, and started to voice these nine-note, ethereal crazy chords. Sly was way back in the bedroom and he came out yelling, 'Who in the fuck is doing that on my organ?' He came in and saw. 'Miles, get your mother-fucking ass out,' he said. 'Don't ever play that voodoo shit here . . . .' Miles left, and I said, 'Sly, that was *Miles Davis* you were talking to.' 'I don't give a fuck,' he said."

Actor, director, and sometime musician Melvin Van Peebles drew a more favorable report from Ria, as a guest with good influence: "He was normal and happy and creative." Sly himself seemed happy in the studio that Columbia had set up in his flat. "It wasn't like the old days [in California], when I could just sit down on the piano bench and listen to him create for hours," Ria sighs. But, "You should have heard the stuff he recorded" at Central Park West. "It's never been released. Hours and hours of beauty. It was funky, good backbeat, it got down. It wasn't mostly fast, hot dance music. It was calmer than that—very intricate and beautiful," perhaps closer to some of his post-*Small Talk* tracks for Epic. Ria, meanwhile, "took over being the Mother Love kind of person around the house," cooking up creamed corn from scratch, as Sly's mother had taught her to do.

There wasn't much evidence of communication with the rest of the Family Stone, though there were long-distance entreaties from Cynthia, fielded by Ria. "She was just begging to be paid. 'Please, please talk to him.' 'I did, Cynthia, I did, yesterday.' Sly didn't have an 'attitude' toward anyone; he was only focused on creating his music." Ria recalls only one instance when Sly's cocaine addiction may have indirectly resulted in some friction between her and him. "I said, 'Who the hell do you think you are, Jesus Christ?' Because he was already having that kind of delusion." After a tense pause, "He looked at me and couldn't stop laughing. And Bubba kind of looked over his shoulder at me and gave me a sign like, he really *does* think he's Jesus Christ, so let's not say that anymore."

You Don't Have to Come Down

— 1972-1974 —

If a man does not keep pace with his companions, perhaps it is because he hears a different drummer. Let him step to the music which he hears, however measured or far away.

—HENRY DAVID THOREAU

I was really tired of R & B sounding the same. I think Sly taught me that. I think that it's important for Black music to always, always grow.

—RICK JAMES

THE LONG WAIT FOR *RIOT* helped it debut at the top of *Bill-board*'s pop charts in 1971, and three of its tracks also charted as singles. The follow-up album, *Fresh*, is seen in retrospect as Sly's last dealings with anything like a major hit. Work on *Fresh*, in 1972 and '73, brought him back to the Bay Area and to his long-ago employer Tom Donahue. Among the other engineers credited on the album are Bob Gratts, Mike

Fusaro, James Green, Family standby Don Puluse, and Tom Flye. The latter had gone west, from New York City to Sausalito, just north of the Golden Gate Bridge, to launch the Record Plant recording studios there. At the point they hooked up, "Sly had recorded [most of] *Fresh*, but he wasn't happy with it, so Donahue said, 'You ought to go to the Plant and see Flye,'" explains Tom, who still lives within a short drive from the Plant. Before his move, he'd briefly worked with Sly in New York. "I mixed his part of the *Woodstock* album, [on which Sly and the group] played very well. And not everybody did."

For *Fresh*, "We rerecorded everything in place on the tape, and we just dubbed over whatever was there. And the way he kept it together, since it was piecemeal—one instrument at a time—was that he had a Rhythm King drum machine. He called it the Funk Box, because there were rhythms that had a groove to them. It was like a glorified click track [the term for a sort of analog electronic metronome]. You could adjust the tempo, and . . . you could pre-set different beats and change them a little bit." An advancement over the preexisting Rhythm Ace, the Maestro Rhythm King gen-erated a sterile, "dry" tone lacking the acoustic properties of a real drum kit but making for its own kind of supple groove.

"[Sly] was so innovative in the process of recording," Tom con-tinues. "He was the first guy to record piecemeal, one track at a time, using this click track. 'Cause quite often, he'd play all the parts," and would need the coordinating guidance of the clicks. "If someone could play it better, fine. But usually he played it better than anybody—everybody except for his brother Freddie." Tom had determined early in his long career to accommodate the recording process as much as possible to his clients' needs. He'd been a professional drummer in the '60s for Don McLean (on the anthemic "American Pie") and for a moderately successful group called Lothar and the Hand People. He'd experienced what it was like to be disrespected by a recording studio (Capitol) and had vowed, "I never want to treat an artist that way."

Adjusting to Sly involved some challenging and fascinating improvisations. Breaking with studio tradition, Sly preferred playing instruments in the control room, usually reserved for engineers and producers, rather than in the studio area proper. "And he liked to sing in the control room, which was kind of a pain in the butt," says Tom. "You get the 'bleed' from the speakers." Sly's earlier recording with the Family Stone had stayed closer to the standard format, "where everybody pretty much played all at the same time, or you'd have the rhythm section and the vocalist and then you'd add the strings or the horns." But once Sly started flying solo, he "did it track–by track, he pulled this together in his head, and it was amazing. He's hearing in his imagination the ultimate product, so he can understand what each individual thing is."

Ken Roberts, replacing the troubled David Kapralik as the band's manager in financially shaky times, had reportedly recommended that the leader divest himself of his players as an unnecessary expense. Although Sly still seems resentful about that suggestion, Tom finds other evidence that the separation from the band bore hidden virtues. Sly, he believes, "could play all the parts better" than any pick-up musician, "and he knew what he wanted, so he didn't have to try to explain it to anyone." Supplying most of the ingredients himself, and replacing a human drummer with a machine, were in Tom's opinion "just a different art form."

Says Tom about the recording of "Babies Makin' Babies," a seeming warning about unwanted pregnancies: "We were working . . . and every time we'd get to this one section of the song, he'd say, 'This is really funky! Those four bars are really funky!' And they were. So he says, 'I sure wish I could have the whole track like

I WANT TO TAKE YOU HIGHER

those four bars.' He'd done a rough vocal, a 'guide' vocal [a dummy track, to be erased later, from which to reference other takes]. So he says, 'Is there any way we could make it all like that?' I said, 'I don't know, but I can try.' We were working on two-inch tape, so I stayed 'after school' that night and made a couple hundred copies of those four bars. . . . And then I took a razor blade and cut them all together. He came in the next day, and really loved it.

"As far as I know, that was one of the first times anybody had made what in reality was a multitrack loop, which nowadays is the basis of how many people make a record. . . . But in the digital domain, you can go in and move 'em around, do whatever you want. With a razor blade, it's a little harder. So it's another thing that [Sly] kind of started. . . . He had a sense of, 'Let's go for it, let's try it.' Engineers are always trying to keep things technically together, so they're often on the careful side. But you also have to let creativity breathe. I'm after the emotional content when I'm recording or mixing . . . and to have someone come in who *exuded* emotional content—," Tom chuckles, "it was great."

Gazing back more than three decades, it's tough for Tom to identify particular tracks on which he was influential, the more so because there was no sure way of keeping track of them. "Sly had gotten ripped off a number of times in his life, and he would not leave the tapes at the studio. He had like a Toyota station wagon, which one of his bodyguards drove, and every night the thing would pull up [to the Record Plant] and they would unload all the tapes. At the end of the [late-night] session, the next day or whatever, they'd pack it back up and take off. Sometimes the paperwork would get lost with the reels of tape, you wouldn't know where the songs were, and sometimes you'd have tracks which were started but didn't have a name for them yet."

Fresh continued to move the sound of Sly's music away from that of a live band and toward what might be dubbed a proto-techno mode. The drum machines, multiple overdubs, and tape loops deployed by Tom were all early, makeshift versions of studio tools that would become ubiquitous in later decades, along with increasing computer sophistication. Still new in 1973, this approach put a hypnotic electronic gloss on *Fresh*, testifying yet again to Sly's innovative pioneering genius. Today, when anyone with a computer and a digital recorder can burn their own music disc, technology has become overextended, to the detriment of pop music generally.

Sly's diminished but ongoing recording and performing activity still needed flesh-and-blood players to go along with the machines. When Jerry Martini began demanding what he saw as fair compensation for past and present services, Sly hired saxophonist Pat Rizzo. Was that the coercion it appeared to be? "I guess you could call it that," Jerry responds. "But I [ended up getting] my money." Actually, Jerry and Pat served Sly together for a while (both men were credited on the sleeve of *Fresh*). They became friends, and they were both present for the return of Sly to the Apollo in Harlem, in March 1972. Brother Freddie was present in body too, but not in spirit. "Freddie passed out at the Apollo," Bubba Banks reported to Joel Selvin. "I think the thing was, who could get the highest and be the most out of it. Freddie was always trying to get Sly's attention. Everybody was trying to out-high each other."

Another sort of competition had Larry Graham attempting to out-macho Sly. Larry's questioning of Sly's authority had surfaced during the first few hours of the band's existence, and it's arguable that his handsome, cocky stage presence, resonant vocals, and peerless bass technique later drew some of the spotlight away from Sly. Behind the scenes, there were reports of affairs with Rose and with Freddie's wife, Sharon. Ultimately, Larry assembled his own posse of brutal, badass hangers-on. By the time of the making of *Riot*, Larry's bass parts were among the countless overdubs requested and sometimes discarded by Sly, who played the instrument himself on "You Caught Me Smilin'." "I didn't play anything with the rest of the band," Larry griped to *Mojo*, and his thump 'n' pluck style is certainly less noticeable on *Riot*.

Late in 1972, Sly and Larry's two sets of "bodyguards" confronted each other at L.A.'s Cavalier Hotel. Bubba Banks and his pal Larry Chin, high on PCP and inspired by a recent screening of Stanley Kubrick's dystopian film *A Clockwork Orange*, assaulted Larry's henchmen Vernon "Moose" Constan and Robert Joyce with fists, feet, and walking sticks. Sly's men had also been assigned to apprehend Larry Graham, over what Sly perceived as the bassist's insubordination and alleged designs on Sly's life. Alerted to the threat, Pat Rizzo sought out Larry and his girlfriend, Patryce, in their hotel room at the Cavalier and escorted them safely away from the mayhem. Later in San Francisco, Ken Roberts could not persuade a shaken Larry, who continued to fear for his life, to rejoin the group.

"Sometimes in a family, it comes time to go," a discreet and reformed Larry told *Bass Player* years later. He went on to form Graham Central Station, and by the time of that group's biggest hit, *One in a Million You* (1980), Larry was better known as a singer than as a bassist. Larry then dissolved his band, but was always sought as an accompanist, and he found gigs with Carlos Santana, Chaka Khan, Aretha Franklin, and Stanley Jordan. He also made a popular instructional video for aspiring bass players, with his oldest and greatest rhythmic teammate Greg Errico serving as drummer.

Sly handpicked a replacement bassist, Rustee Allen, who'd been pointed out by Larry himself. The young Louisiana native, now a resident of Oakland, had experience playing with blues guitarist Johnny Talbot, the Edward Hawkins singers, and Vet Stone's Little Sister group. Rustee fit in quickly on *Fresh*, most memorably pouring out the haunting bass line on "If You Want Me to Stay." "Rather than being controlling, [Sly] encouraged the tune's spirit and vibe," Rustee told *Bass Player*. "He wanted me to be myself and put my nuances in the part." Influenced more by Motown stalwart James Jamerson's melodic technique than by Larry's percussive snap, the new recruit managed to blend the two. "Although I've always been primarily a finger-style player, I was able to adapt," he pointed out. "It's sort of a light slap in which you hold your thumb perpendicular to the strings and, using just the side of your thumb, you strike the string, sometimes using a little bit of your nail. You control the notes' duration with your left hand." The effect helped morph Sly's sound from psychedelic funk toward studio-rigged soul.

Seeking another real live drummer, Sly went with Pat Rizzo's recommendation of Andy Newmark, a solid pro with extensive credentials in a variety of acts. The Drumming World Web site has described how Andy was introduced to the leader of the Family Stone while Sly was prone and zoned-out in bed. "Are you funky?" Sly managed to ask. Andy replied in the affirmative, and sat down at a nearby kit to play for less than a minute. It was all Sly needed to command Freddie to replace Greg's temporary replacement, Jerry Gibson. Widely considered one of the Family Stone's most valuable additions, Andy later went on to play with David Bowie,

George Benson, Luther Vandross, and with John Lennon on his final album, *Double Fantasy*.

Riot's one big hit had been "Family Affair." For *Fresh*, released in 1973, it was "If You Want Me to Stay" (revived thirty-four years later as a highlight of Sly's comeback performances). It's a slinky mid-tempo soul statement, based on the same Phrygian mode of chord changes as Bobby Hebb's 1966 hit "Sunny." Rustee recalled for *Bass Player* Sly's reaction to his freestyling fretwork on his Fender Jazz bass: "He just turned his back to me and grooved with my interpretation, giving a shout when he really liked what he heard," which involved nailing down the rhythm while pumping out flourishes of eighth- and sixteenth-note fills, effectively functioning as the track's lead instrument. Andy Newmark's drums propelled the song unobtrusively. "I didn't zero in on any part of his kit per se," Rustee explained. "I just focused on the overall groove."

Among the most distinctive of the tracks was the disc's opener, "In Time," spiraling out in a treacherous time signature that one-upped "Thank You (Falletinme Be Mice Elf Agin)." Miles Davis was reportedly so struck by this piece that he made his band listen to it repeatedly, to absorb its snakelike syncopation. The remaining songs were arguably somewhat brighter and more artful than *Riot*'s, with something of the sensuality of Al Green or Marvin Gaye and an obvious influence on the later output of Stevie Wonder. Equally upbeat was the cover art, featuring images by fine art/fashionista photographer Richard Avedon of a grinning Sly (again without ensemble), high-kicking in a tight leather outfit, bare-chested, and sporting a lush Afro. Compared to *Riot*, the album was also embedded with more "message" material. "Let Me Have It All" carried an almost gospel hopefulness, supported by wah-wah guitar, bubbly bass, and female chorus. "Thankful N'

The Stewart Family
Four siblings (plus
littlest sister Vaetta)
gathered in gospel
garb at their Denio
Street homestead in
Vallejo, California,
in 1952. From left:
Vaetta (Vet),
Frederick (Freddie),
Rose, Sylvester
(Sly, age nine), and
Loretta. (Courtesy
of Edwin and Arno
Konings.)

The Viscaynes singing
group, out of Vallejo
High School, posed
in a promotional shot
for their early '60s
single "Uncle Sam
Needs You." Sly
Stewart kneels in
front of (from left)
Frank Arellano, Vern
Gebhardt, Charlie
Gebhardt, Charlene
Imhoff, and Maria
(Ria) Boldway
Douglas. The photo
was taken by Ria's
father, John, at the
Gebhardts'. (Courtesy
of Maria Boldway
Douglas.)

Sly sat in as producer, pianist, and more at a December 1966 Autumn Records recording session for the Great Society. Also pictured (from left) are Rachel Donahue, "Big Tom" Donahue, pianist Billy Preston (seated on sofa), and Autumn promo man Dick Forester. (Courtesy of Alec Palao.)

A few weeks after their formation, Sly (on keyboards) & the Family Stone brought in New Year 1967 at Winchester Cathedral in Redwood City, California. Other band members visible (from left) are Greg Errico (drums), Cynthia Robinson (trumpet), Jerry Martini (sax), and Freddie Stone (doubling on horn). (Courtesy of the Neal Austinson Archives.)

Doing their best to tout their 1967 debut album for Epic, *A Whole New Thing*, were (from left) Greg Errico, Sly Stone, Cynthia Robinson, Freddie Stone, Larry Graham, and Jerry Martini. (Courtesy of the Neal Austinson Archives.)

The Family Stone, in this promo shot for a 1968 issue of *Life,* was in full force, with (from left) Freddie Stone, Sly Stone, Rose Stone, Larry Graham, Cynthia Robinson, Jerry Martini, and Greg Errico. (Courtesy of the Neal Austinson Archives.)

Manager David Kapralik made use of an image from *The Ed Sullivan Show* and Sly's reputation as "incredible and unpredictable" to assemble this ad for *Billboard* in 1969. (Courtesy of the Neal Austinson Archives.)

On the same day in December 1969 that they showcased their Afros and their funk-rock power on *The Ed Sullivan Show*, the Family Stone lined up for Epic. This photo, attributed to Stephen Paley, also appeared on the cover of *Rolling Stone*. (Courtesy of the Neal Austinson Archives.)

Sly wasn't quite ready for the Monterey Pop Festival in 1967, but two years later, he was featured at that same location with the Family Stone, as one of the few rock acts included in the Monterey Jazz Festival. (Photo by Baron Wolman.)

Among the many rock and pop stars ascending to legend status at the Woodstock Music and Arts Fair, Sly & the Family Stone shone as one of the best and brightest, in the early hours of August 16, 1969. (Photo by Jim Marshall.)

Sly flashed peace vees during ABC's *In Concert* in November 1973. Though Sly was not strictly an activist, the positive messages in some of his lyrics and the affirmative appearance of the multiethnic Family Stone band had positioned him comfortably within the Love Generation, for a while. (Photo by Jim Marshall.)

Jim Marshall featured this portrait of Sly, performing in San Jose in 1973, in his book of rock shots, *Not Fade Away* (Wolfgang's Vault). In the accompanying caption, Marshall, himself a rock legend, declared, "Sly Stone is one of the most charismatic performers I've met. He could light up a concert hall with a smile." (Photo by Jim Marshall.)

For ABC's *In Concert,* Sly (at the keyboard) was accompanied by Lucy Hambrick, Tiny Mouton, and Vet Stone (as Little Sister), as well as Freddie Stone (guitar) and Rustee Allen (bass). (Courtesy of the Neal Austinson Archives.)

Far ahead of the purveyors of glam rock and such image-conscious icons as David Bowie and Elton John, Sly carefully chose the details of his wardrobe and accessories, including eyewear and wigs. This was taken in L.A. in 1973. (Courtesy of the Neal Austinson Archives.)

Some of the most accessible and sympathetic portraits of Sly were captured by Stephen Paley, first a photographer for, and later an executive at, Columbia Records. This was taken at the Beverly Hills home of Columbia president Clive Davis in the early 1970s. (Photo by Stephen Paley.)

Sharing the after-gig glow in a Manhattan hotel suite with Sly and Freddie (behind Sly, with glasses) were the Family Stone's manager, David Kapralik (at left), and the William Morris Agency's Al DeMarino (at right). (Courtesy of Sony Archives/The Selvin Collection.)

Columbia A & R man Stephen Paley (left), in a dressing room at Madison Square Garden, talked about his role as best man just before Sly's wedding at that venue to Kathy Silva on June 5, 1974. (From the collection of Stephen Paley.)

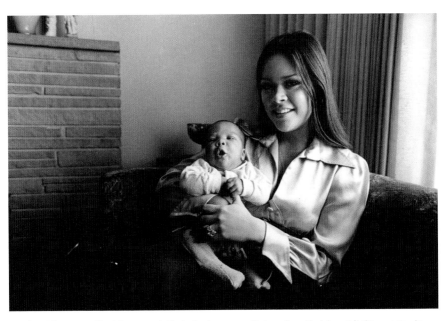

Kathy Silva cradled her and Sly's baby son, Sylvester Bubba Ali Stewart, Jr., at aunt Rose Banks' home in Oakland, early 1974. (Photo by Jim Marshall.)

Sly made several memorable TV appearances as guest and co-host on *The Mike Douglas Show* in 1974. (Courtesy of the Neal Austinson Archives.)

To help signal that he was living up to the title of his *Back on the Right Track* album in 1979, Warner Bros. pictured Sly in three-piece establishment finery, the image of supposed financial and personal health. (Courtesy of the Neal Austinson Archives.)

Sly made his last recording for Warner Bros. in 1982 and made a few appearances at the Keystone clubs around the Bay Area, including this one in Berkeley. But his fans would soon lose touch with him for a couple of decades. (Courtesy of the Neal Austinson Archives.)

With Hamp "Bubba" Banks (right), his sometime role model, companion, brother-in-law, associate producer, and intimate personal assistant, Sly trod the tarmac of LAX in 1972. (Photo by Jim Marshall.)

Though long hidden from the public eye, Sly (left) continued writing and recording music privately. This shot from the late 1980s finds him in the Crystal Recording Studio in Hollywood beside his controversial manager Jerry Goldstein (center) and helpmate Lou Gordon (right). (Courtesy of Lou Gordon.)

Siblings Freddie and Rose, who'd been harmonizing since childhood, reunited at the mike in 2003. (Photo by Stephen Paley.)

Greg Errico contributed to several attempts at recapturing the Family Stone legacy, including the 2003 sessions in L.A. (as shown here). Over three decades, he also served as producer (and sometime drummer) for funk diva Betty Davis and big band vocalist Jamie Davis (no relation). (Photo by Stephen Paley.)

Settling in Southern California, Rose Stone maintained a career as a studio vocalist into the new millennium and recorded a solo album. With her daughter Lisa, Rose joined her brother Sly on some of his comeback gigs. (Photo by Stephen Paley.)

After decades away from the spotlight, Sly showed up for the Grammys' tribute to him and the Family Stone at the Staples Center in L.A. on February 8, 2006. He didn't sing or play much, but made an indelible visual impression with a blonde Mohawk adhered to his scalp. (©Lucy Nicholson/Reuters/Corbis.)

On January 13, 2007, Sly broke a two-decade hiatus from public performance with a gig at the House of Blues in Anaheim, California, sporting the stick-on Mohawk he'd worn during a Grammy tribute a year earlier. At his hotel after the gig, he hung with brothers Edwin (left) and Arno Konings, superfans and biographers who'd flown in from Holland with a documentary film crew. (Courtesy of Edwin and Arno Konings.)

Capping a year of performing with a variety of younger ensembles and a couple of veterans under the Family Stone moniker, Sly played the B. B. King Blues Club and Grill in Manhattan in November and December 2007. Pictured backstage are (in the rear) road manager Neal Austinson and vocalist Rikki Gordon, (kneeling in front) drummer Stephan Dubose, (standing, from left) keyboardist Tony Stead, trumpeter Cynthia Robinson, saxophonist Jerry Martini, guitarist and musical director Tony Yates, Sly, trombonist Mike Rinta, vocalist Lisa Stone Banks, and bassist Pete Yates. (Courtesy of Rikki Gordon.)

Sly's return to performance in 2007 included a European tour, which placed him and a newly configured band here at the North Sea Jazz Festival in Rotterdam. Reactions of press and public were mixed. (Photo by Rob Verhorst/Redferns.)

Thoughtful" showcased Cynthia's tight trumpeting in a similarly bright vein. Here was evidence that, musically at least, Sly was not on the steady road to hell to which many seemed ready to consign him.

Aside from its single hit, *Fresh* is probably best remembered for Sly's haunting, sincere arrangement of Doris Day's standard "Que Sera, Sera (Whatever Will Be, Will Be)." This rare (for Sly) cover was intoned by Rose, with Sly on chorus, in a slow-swaying, praise-giving manner evocative of their childhood harmonizing in church. The reflective song had been penned by Ray Evans and Jay Livingston, and first heard in Alfred Hitchcock's 1956 film *The Man Who Knew Too Much*, but its inclusion on *Fresh* resulted in a controversy having nothing to do with music or movies. The cover had been facilitated by Sly's good-time Hollywood hang partner and Doris's son, Terry Melcher. The friends didn't anticipate that they were spawning an urban legend, persisting for decades: that Sly Stone had slept with Doris Day.

It was probably a collective projection of sexual fantasies about the perky singer-turned-actress Doris, common among American males of the '50s and '60s. Today, David Kapralik and Steve Paley are both ready to put the myth to rest. "I was Terry Melcher's mentor at Columbia, and we became good friends and remained so through the years," says David. "I introduced Sly to Terry, and several times Terry joined me at Sly's recording sessions. I often visited with Terry and Doris at their home in Beverly Hills, and one day I brought Sly with me to hang out with Terry." "Sly was mainly interested in buying one of her cars," Steve continues. "Sly did go to Doris's house, but only to see the car in question, and that's when Terry introduced him to his mother."

"They had a brief conversation, and then Doris went into the kitchen," David goes on. "While she was out of the room, Sly went to the piano in the living room and began to play 'Que Sera, Sera.' Then Doris came out of the kitchen, on her way elsewhere in the house, and with Sly accompanying her, she sang a few bars of the song." Steve describes their rendition as "a gospel version," not unlike its delivery on *Fresh*. "To the best of my knowledge, that is the first and last time Sly and Doris met," attests David, "despite the false and scurrilous tabloid reports that appeared subsequently." "After the song came out, that stupid Sly–Doris Day rumor started," concludes Steve. "It amused Sly at the time, but irritated Doris. Part of the reason this rumor took hold was because Doris was supposedly having an affair with Maury Wills, a black L.A. Dodgers baseball player," an item attested to in Wills's 1991 autobiography.

During and after the making of *Fresh*, Tom Flye's engineering engagement with Sly continued, and expanded beyond the studio. "I did a bunch of television shows, I even went out and did front-of-the-house [at concerts] for him sometimes," says the engineer. "We basically kind of lived together for a while. He had a studio in L.A., he had a studio in New York, and at CBS. We spent a lot of time together, because he recorded every day. Sometimes I'd take my mobile unit over to his mother's house [in San Francisco] and we'd record in the basement."

Sly manifested more admiration and trust with Tom, whom he'd dubbed "Superflye," than with most studio personnel. "There were rumors all over the industry," says Tom, "that he'd shot up control rooms, yelled at engineers, all kinds of stuff. But he treated me like a king. We just got along. I think he realized that I was trying to help, I wasn't just there for my paycheck . . . and he liked the results, the way it sounded." When Sly was late for a recording session or anticipated not showing, he'd phone Tom from his vehicle, on a cumbersome early model pre-cell portable phone. And

Sly confided that Tom had been the first white man whom his mother, Alpha, had allowed entrance to her home unescorted by one of her offspring. (Frank Arellano had been afforded that privilege years earlier, but he could claim mixed race). "I think [Alpha] got the sense that I wasn't there to rip her son off, that I was there to try to help," says Tom.

In turn, Tom maintained his diligence in catering to his client's whims and demands. "I remember we were at the Record Plant, and he was doing a guitar part. He got about half of it done, and he said, 'You know, I really wanted to use my new guitar. The problem is, it's in L.A. Let's go to L.A.'" Tom continues: "We pack up, we go. So I get the song and say, 'You wanna start at the top?' He says, 'No, no, let's just punch in where we were at.' I say, 'It's a different guitar, Sly, it's gonna sound different.' He says, 'That's okay, just do it.' So we do it, and it turns out to be a really unique change in the song. The first [guitar] was real clean-sounding, like a jazz guitar, and then the guitar in L.A. sounded more rock 'n' rollish, more distorted. . . . You gotta take things and work them to your advantage." (Though Sly as a guitarist was associated with the jangly Fender Telecaster, in the period of *Riot*, and after, he'd taken to using the fatter-sounding Gibson Les Paul in the studio and onstage. He had both these instruments custom decorated with swirling adornments.)

Among Sly's paramours after *Riot* and during the making of *Fresh* was Kathy Silva, a lovely Hawaiian-born aspiring actress and model about ten years his junior. She'd romanced him in the company of her older sister, April, and had befriended Maria Boldway during Ria's last stay with Sly. In 1973, Kathy bore Sly a son, Sylvester Bubba Ali Stewart Jr., and the common-law family of three posed for the cover of *Small Talk*, released the following year.

In that photo, and in the record's concept and execution, it almost seemed as if the high-kicking, high-living rock rioter was ready to come down to earth. Some of *Small Talk*'s material celebrated love and family life: "Mother Beautiful," "This Is Love," and the title tune. Casual studio conversation was audible between and during the pieces. There were classical trappings (solo violinist Sid Page was credited as a Family member) and contributions from old friends, including Rose, Freddie, Jerry, and little sister Vet, as well as more recent helpmates Pat Rizzo, Rustee Allen, and drummer Bill Lordan, who'd replaced both Andy Newmark and (temporarily) Sly's drum machines.

Bill, later to find longtime high-profile work with British bluesrocker Robin Trower, described for the Trower Web site his enlistment into Sly's band in 1973: "I was at Paramount Studios on Santa Monica Boulevard in Los Angeles, waiting to meet Bobby Womack. Sly walked into the studio with his entire entourage [and] one of the bodyguards, Bubba Banks, who was Sly's sister Rose's husband, came out of the studio and asked if I was a drummer, because he had seen me sitting there with sticks in my hand. . . . He asked me if I would like to come in and play on some tracks that Sly was working on at the time. I said that I would. . . . So, I went into the studio with Bubba, where I met Sly, and Sly told me to 'Go out behind the drums and put on the headphones and see what you can come up with.' There were two songs that night, 'Livin' While I'm Livin'' and 'Say You Will,' which are both on the *Small Talk* album, which I later recorded with Sly. When the [first] track came to an end, I looked up and saw that in the control room there was all this commotion. So I got up from the drums and went in to see what was up. That's when Sly turned to me and said, 'You are in the Family Stone.' I got the job, but I didn't know that I was auditioning for Sly, who did not have a regular, full-time drummer at the time. He needed somebody to do both studio and live shows."

Bill credited Sly with enhancing both his career and his technique. "He gave me his concept of how to interpret his uncanny sense of rhythm," said the drummer. "He always called me 'Lord.' He said, 'Lord, play sloppy tight and raggedy clean.' Then Sly sat down behind my drums and showed me what he meant. . . . It was kind of a disjointed, loose, but tight placement of the beats on the drums. It was how he placed the kick drum and snare that was unlike the way a 'normal' drummer would play it, but made so much sense, and he was very musical. Then when he got up from the drums, he'd tell me to take what he'd showed me and put my 'polish' on it. . . . Sly was most intrigued with a drum beat I came up with that we later titled 'Stick 'n' Lick.' We worked on it at the Record Plant in Sausalito. We just laid down a backing track of it, without any words. The groove was an inspiration from listening to Jabo Starks, who was the original drummer for James Brown." Bill testified about his later tours with Sly, through 1973 and '74: "Sometimes we were playing live, I thought we were the greatest band in the world. . . . Sly helped me to develop my own sense of what was unique."

Engineer Tom Flye further confirms that Sly remained a musical innovator, eager to avoid some of the conceits of production. "He liked a real tight sound. . . . He liked to hear instruments come and go [in recording], he didn't want them to hang around. . . . He didn't like a lot of reverb. A lot of records (for your everyday listener who doesn't realize how they're made) sound like they're recorded in a huge room, Carnegie Hall or something like that. Vocals hang on like it's in a cavern. . . . [But Sly] didn't want that kind of stuff."

A small helping of Sly Jr.'s fretful baby sounds and Kathy's coo-ing made it into *Small Talk*'s mix, on the album's opening title tune, a couple of years ahead of Stevie Wonder's similar, far more celebrated paternal nod on "Isn't She Lovely." In a contrasting mood, the harmony vocals, keening horns, and Rustee's propul-sive bass on "Loose Booty" sparked with erotic potency. The song's lyric chant was later adapted by white rappers the Beastie Boys for their "Shadrach." Also influential, as a soul music cliché, was the pouring of Sid Page's syrupy strings over Freddie's undulating gui-tar on several tracks, including "Say You Will," "Mother Beautiful," "Time for Livin'," and "Holdin' On." (Similar sounds are found on B. B. King's "The Thrill Is Gone" and the Temptations' "Papa Was a Rollin' Stone.") The slow ballad "Wishful Thinkin' " evinced Sly's early introduction to jazz by David Froehlich, with authentically smoky guitar that echoed the style of Barney Kessel or Herb Ellis. "Livin' While I'm Livin' " was a session of hard-driving chase music, "This Is Love" felt like an homage to the '50s doo-wop with which Sly had begun his career with the Viscaynes back in Vallejo. And the final track, "Can't Strain My Brain," resonated with a bluesy appeal evocative of "If You Want Me to Stay." Sly's own compositional and arranging uniqueness were perhaps less in evi-dence on *Small Talk* than on his prior Epic sides, and the partici-pation of Family Stone veterans didn't result in an identifiable revival of the band's sound. But the album still stands higher than many other artists' best efforts. "Time for Livin' " managed to get a hold, weaker than Sly and the band's previous efforts, at number 32 on the hit parade.

After *Small Talk*, Sly began to drift away from engineer Tom Flye, but he continued his connection with the Record Plant. "Basically, he was living on budget. When he'd need some money, he'd finish a record and turn it in," Tom observes. "One of the owners of the Record Plant talked him into building a studio in the back area of the building, which we called 'the Pit.' Traditionally, there's a studio, and the control room is a bit higher, so [the engineers, producers, and other technicians] see down into the studio. . . . But I remember [Sly] saying, 'Why can't we sink the control room down?'. So the control room was sunk down in the middle, and there were areas all around where he could have the amplifiers and drums and such. . . . They made him a bedroom and a bathroom, so he could go back there and do what he wanted to do."

Alec Palao, not a fan of Sly's recorded output during this period, hazards a guess at what Sly and his studio supporters wanted to do in the Pit. "Probably, for every month he was there, three weeks would be drug taking and partying, and there might be one week of attempts at recording music," opines Alec.

Tom can't recall nefarious business in the Pit, but he also doesn't know if Sly ever recorded anything there that made it onto a record. Sly's unusual studio configuration was maintained at the Record Plant long after he had returned to recording in his own abode and elsewhere. The Pit was rented out to other artists, including Rolling Stones bassist Bill Wyman. Despite the money invested in Sly, and the time and effort he was investing in studios commercial and personal, his own shelf life seemed to be coming into question.

COLUMBIA/CBS HAD BEEN ANTEING up over a half-million dollars in advance for each of Sly's last few successful recording projects, but the company offered something less for *Small Talk*, because its predecessor, *Fresh*, had sold less than previous Sly & the Family Stone albums had. With his career in apparent need of bolstering, Sly decided, in dialogue with his long-term trusted friend CBS's Steve Paley, to make a media event out of his marriage to girlfriend and co-parent Kathy Silva. The public ceremony would bestow familial legitimacy on Sly Jr., already known to fans from the *Small Talk* cover.

Steve Paley recalls that Irwin Siegelstein, who'd replaced Clive Davis at CBS, allotted some $25,000 for Sly's wedding party, scheduled for June 5, 1974, at Madison Square Garden, the scene of some of the Family Stone's best-remembered performances in New York City. There would also be a wedding reception at the Starlight Room of the Waldorf-Astoria. Steve engaged celebrated fashion designer Halston (with Sly reportedly paying the bill) to clothe Sly and Kathy, their mothers, all Sly's siblings, the other members of the Family Stone and Little Sister groups, Bubba Banks, an additional personal assistant nicknamed Buddha, and a dozen black models, serving as a sort of collective flower girl but bearing gilded palms instead of blossoms. To Freddie Stone's disappointment, Steve was designated best man.

The wedding gig produced the expected and much-needed media attention for Sly, but not necessarily in the tone that Steve would have preferred. Maureen Orth, in *Newsweek*, characterized Sly as "one of the shrewdest and highest-paid talents in the pop world," and declared that he'd "always been the badass of the rock world." She described the wedding scene as a performance before "23,000 screaming freaks." Steve later confided to Joel Selvin that Sly had attempted to seduce Maureen on the evening of the event. George W. S. Trow, a writer friend of Steve's, provided a more sympathetic and detailed—though sardonic—account for the *New Yorker* magazine. He portrayed Sly as "a lean, graceful man with a large smile" and went on to state, "He is in control of his leanness and his grace. He is in control of his large smile. He is in control of many of the people around him, and, sporadically, he is in control of his considerable talent." Accompanying Steve on a premarital visit to Sly's Central Park West flat and waiting to take the star to a fitting at Halston's, George was inspired to comment, "Sly uses small, benign delays in the way that a lion uses small, undeadly nips to indicate affection while calling attention to his teeth." One virtue of Sly's particular talent, the writer observed, is: "A singer who appeals to hip blacks and hip whites at the same time makes a lot of money." But about the purported evolution of the ideals of the '60s into the harsher realities of the '70s, George felt that "the waited-for convergence of white and black experience on the countercultural grid failed to take place." Of Ken Roberts, who attended and helped plan the wedding, George wrote, "He became Sly's manager in 1972, at a time when Sly was very badly behaved, when, Roberts says, no one else wanted the job. He books Sly's concerts and exercises some tactical control, but he seems to have few long-term ambitions for Sly. While Paley (who is almost Sly's age) and others at Epic Records seem eager to make a new career for Sly, Roberts seems willing to ride the old one out."

The Madison Square Garden wedding, then, was conceived as an entertaining and hopefully regenerative part of Steve's script, not Ken's. Playing the role of master of ceremonies was Don Cornelius, immaculate host of TV's syndicated music program *Soul Train*. Geraldo Rivera was billed as both celebrity reporter and "eyewitness usher." By Maureen Orth's reckoning, though, the "Family Affair for 23,000" never lived up to the planning and expectations. "Security guards," she noted, "wouldn't let Sly and his bride march down the aisle. The Humane Society called and said they'd arrest [set designer and de facto wedding director Joe] Eula if he released 500 white doves in the Garden. . . . And Tom Donahue, the 400-pound disc jockey who was originally supposed to perform the ceremony, had to bow out because he wasn't ordained in New York State," although mail-order ordinations were readily available. The Garden service was in fact performed by B. R. Stewart, ordained as a Bay Area–based bishop in the Church of God in Christ, the sect in which Sly's mother, Alpha, had been raised in Denton, Texas. After listening to a timely musical rendition of "Family Affair," the audience became energized, and mama Alpha took the mike to remind them that her son's nuptials were "a sacred ceremony." The service was followed by a secular Family Stone concert, which for Maureen, at least, "showed Sly's lack of preparation with his band." Then came the reception, to which Sly was conveyed in "his brand-new $38,000 brown Mercedes limo, one of a dozen cars he owns." Select guests at the reception included New York Philharmonic conductor Leonard Bernstein's daughter Jamie, Judy Garland's daughter Lorna Luft, and pop artist Andy Warhol.

Looking back on all the hoopla, Steve now admits that "it didn't do anything for record sales." George, in the *New Yorker*, drolly closed his piece by noting, "Sly's new album, *Small Talk*, has picked up some momentum on the charts. Currently, it is thirty-nine on *Billboard*'s list, up from forty-nine." But Steve insists that the wedding did in fact "establish Sly as a mainstream artist again. He was asked to host the *Mike Douglas Show* for a week, and he could have done soundtracks, had he a manager that had any kind of foresight. . . . If he'd had [record mogul] David Geffen or someone like that, or even David Kapralik, he would have known how to take advantage of the spotlight that was back on him."

For a while, Sly's career seemed more solid than his marriage. Kathy sued Sly for divorce in November 1974, less than six months after the wedding, complaining he had abducted Sly Jr., among other misdeeds. "He beat me, held me captive, and wanted me to be in a ménage à trois," Kathy confessed to *People* magazine in 1996. "I didn't want that world of drugs and weirdness." But their relationship continued on for several years. "He'd write me a song or promise to change, and I'd try again. We were always fighting, then getting back together." One painful source of conflict was Kathy's discovery that Sly had fathered a daughter, Sylvette Phunne, with his bandmate Cynthia, in 1976. Later that year, Sly's favored fighting dog, Gunn, lacerated Sly Jr.'s scalp at the couple's rented mansion in Novato, in Northern California. Their divorce was finalized after a long estrangement, and Sly was commanded to provide child support, for which noncompliance put him in legal trouble several times. "Sly never grew out of drugs," said Kathy. "He lost his backbone and destroyed his future."

Ever Catch
a Falling Star?

— 1974-2001 —

I've just got to get out. Maybe to Venus or somewhere. Someplace you won't be able to find me.

—JIMI HENDRIX

Funk is to do the best you can and then leave it alone. You can truly say, "Funk it!" 'cause you did the best you can. You don't have to be guilty.

—GEORGE CLINTON
1994 interview with Jeff Kaliss

HOWEVER MUCH HIS PER-sonal life and his performing and recording prospects would later dim, Sly looked pretty good under TV lights. Appearing on *The Mike Douglas Show* a month prior to the Madison Square Garden spectacle, he offered up a solo piano rendition of "If You Want Me to Stay," which exquisitely showed off the harmonic structure of the song, as well as its creator's accomplished keyboard technique.

A month after the wedding, Sly returned as Mike's co-host. The microphone seemed to like Sly's radio-trained, hip baritone voice, the camera liked his large smile and fantastic wardrobe, and Sly seemed comfortable seated beside Mike, a change from the hot seat he'd shared with TV host Dick Cavett three and four years earlier. Douglas and Stone were an act that could appeal even to daytime suburban housewives. Among the show's guests, Sly played particularly well off Muhammad Ali and the Smothers brothers, who were comfortable in themselves and felt no need to compete for attention.

But off-camera, Sly became further distanced from what remained of his original bandmates. The Family Stone was booked, alongside Kool & the Gang, for the better part of a week in January 1975 at Radio City Music Hall in New York, but the booking drew fractional audiences to the 6000-seat venue. There was much grumbling among band members about inadequate transportation, accommodation, and other matters, and mumblings throughout the audience that Robert "Kool" Bell and his Jersey City–based up-and-comers had blown the West Coast hippies off the stage. In short, it was a bumpy lowering of the lifestyle and adulation to which Sly and his band had become accustomed at the beginning of the decade. John Rockwell of the *New York Times* pronounced the concert as "totally out of touch with recession realities," and then elaborated: "Worst of all was the quality of Sly's music. In the not-too-distant past, Sly was one of the most exciting and significant forces in American pop music. But now he has taken to the stalest of rehashes of his greatest hits, ignoring his most recent work, submerging the communal energies of his band under a silly ego trip and rushing perfunctorily through the music he does play. It would be easy to dismiss Sly out of hand. Except that the memories of what he used to be make one more sad than angry."

Cynthia lamented to Joel Selvin about this period: "Not having rehearsals began to take a toll on my playing." Soon after, she said, "I just stopped getting calls for gigs" from Sly. Bubba Banks, still married to Rose, noted to Joel that his wife and other members of the band had "come from three or four thousand [dollars]" for their former shows "to two hundred and fifty" at Radio City. "And I say, 'Rose won't be getting that—we outta here. I took Rose.'" Jerry recalls that Ken Roberts had told him, "I really like you, Jerry, but I don't think Sly really needs you. I think he can just hire a band." Sly's brother, Freddie, reportedly took his frustration about Radio City out on Ken, physically. It was Ken, though, who put up the money for Jerry to get home to California after the show. Sly had left them all in the lurch.

Later in 1975, Sly made an appearance on TV during the *American Music Awards*, but little else was seen of him. In November, he released his first post-Family Epic album, *High on You*. Joel recounts how Sly, while recording the album with a "square john" CBS engineer named Roy Segal in San Francisco, had "set up a tent in the studio. So, when he needs to be 'inspired' he goes into the tent," as if to say, "'I'm not gonna do blow around this cracker.'" Sly's widest exposure that year may have been in a *Playboy* feature, which predictably celebrated the waning artist's still-luxurious and licentious existence. In the Summer of 1976, Sly flew to the Sunshine Festival in Hawaii, and he appeared on two TV specials in the latter part of the year. In December, he released *Heard Ya Missed Me, Well I'm Back* on the Epic label, but it failed to get Sly back on the charts. His *Back on the Right Track*, for Warner Bros. in 1979, managed to chart, but no higher than number 152. During the Warner period, there had been one TV appearance, on *The Midnight Special*, and a San Francisco news spot, both in 1977. Reflecting a few years later, Sly said to journalist Michael

Goldberg, "If you think about it, what could I do after '[I Want to Take You] Higher' or 'If You Want Me to Stay'? I wanted to go fishing, man. Or drive my own car. For a long time, I didn't understand anywhere but hotel rooms, the inside of airplanes, and trying to figure out a way that I didn't come off wrong to human beings."

Over time, benefited by the recent re-releases in CD format, the albums Sly recorded after the breakup of the Family Stone have been more clearly valued. *High on You*, ascribed to Sly Stone and not to any backing band, has been praised as a prime chunk of mid-'70s funk, whose title track made it to number 3 on the R & B charts. *Heard Ya Missed Me*, supported by a "new" Family that included Cynthia and Vet Stewart, and featuring ascending blond guitar angel Peter Frampton on the "Let's Be Together" track, maintained a perhaps deceptive upbeat mood. *Back on the Right Track* packed a funky punch with the hard-hitting "Who's to Say" and "Remember Who You Are," the latter jointly credited to Sly and Bubba Banks. In 1982, Sly created *Ain't But the One Way*, also for Warner, with lyrics engagingly reflective of his wit and of the sort of insightful wisdom he should better have applied to himself. Even his cover (rare for him) of the Kinks' "You Really Got Me," and "Ha Ha, Hee Hee," his bandmate Pat Rizzo's songwriting contribution (another rarity), are distinct and imaginative. *Back on the Right Track* had garnered a number 31 spot on the R & B charts in 1979, and its "Remember Who You Are" rated number 38 among R & B singles. But *Ain't But the One Way* didn't hit, and there was no successful follow-up in the '80s. Sly continued to flicker in the public eye in two different lights: as the source of occasional news flashes about his misdeeds, and as the inspiration, with his now-extinct Family Stone, for a thriving crop of music makers.

Earth, Wind & Fire, Maurice White's audacious and artful blend of mysticism and soul, had already mounted mammoth stage shows and hits like "Shining Star" and "Serpentine Fire." The Commodores, boasting the superb pop sensibility of vocalist and songwriter Lionel Richie, were evolving from the dance boogie of "Slippery When Wet" and "I Feel Sanctified" to slower love songs like "Three Times a Lady" and "Sail On." Kool & the Gang suggested the influence of the band they'd once bested at Radio City, with the infectious funk singles "Celebration" and "Get Down on It." All these acts confirmed the viability of Sly and his band's formula of concocting pop from soul and R & B ingredients, and of manifesting (as long as possible) a fixed group identity. It was a vital change from the older Motown or Stax-Volt studio concoctions, with their contracted, offstage songwriters.

GEORGE CLINTON HELPED TO KEEP Sly both stoned and musically active during some parts of the '80s. George was founder and mastermind of Parliament-Funkadelic, a loose but productive project operating under George's highly—in all senses of the word—conceptual direction. P-Funk had served up a righteous mix of psychedelia and R & B, not unlike some of what was served up by the Family Stone. By the mid-'70s, they'd taken theatrical costumed rock well beyond the Family, in live appearances that were more spectacles than concerts and on hardcore funk albums like *Maggot Brain* and *Mothership Connection*. Guitarist Eddie Hazell sounded like an even more acidified Jimi Hendrix, and rubbery bassist Bootsy Collins seemed heir apparent to Larry Graham. "He's my idol, forget all that 'peer' stuff," George testified to the *Washington Post* in 2006 about Sly. "I heard *Stand!* and it was like: man, forget it! That band was perfect. And Sly was like all the Beatles and all of Motown in one."

While soliciting his idol's presence on his new disc *The Electric Spanking of War Babies* in August 1981, George was arrested with Sly in Los Angeles, for freebasing cocaine in a car. It was neither Sly's first nor last brush with the law. He'd been arrested and placed on probation for coke possession in 1973, and in 1979 had been sued by the IRS for nonpayment of back taxes and put in rehab in lieu of criminal charges after another coke arrest.

In February 1982, Ken Roberts resigned as Sly's manager. Throughout the coming months, Sly tried showcasing his greatest hits with a newly assembled, Georgia-based incarnation of the Family Stone, but his efforts were drawing increasingly jaundiced scrutiny. In San Francisco, there were reports of his forgetting lyrics and switching abruptly from song to song, confusing the band. In Toronto, after taking a fifteen-minute break, Sly returned to the stage to perform "I Want to Take You Higher" without realizing that the other players had already left the stage. The reviewer for the *Toronto Globe and Mail* summed up the audience reaction: "Some of the people leaving the bar following Sly Stone's abortive concert at the Nickelodeon last night (his second this week) were calling the show a rip-off. It wasn't that so much as it was embarrassing and sad." In July 1982, after being busted for cocaine at the Westwood Plaza Hotel in L.A., Sly identified himself as his brother, Freddie.

Through the rest of the decade, Sly accumulated a rap sheet that spanned the continent and a variety of charges. He was arrested in 1983 for possession of a sawed-off shotgun in Illinois. In Florida, he was variously charged with grand theft, welching on a hotel bill, and drug possession. In California, in 1986, he was apprehended for nonpayment of child support (to Kathy) and for possession of coke. In the press, Sly was gaining a different kind of celebrity, as a scoff-law. He was photographed asleep at a court hearing ("Are we keeping you awake?" the judge asked sardonically), he skipped bail after his L.A. coke arrest, and he in general managed to remain elusive, so that certain of his indiscretions took years to catch up with him.

In the time-honored tradition of celebrities, Sly passed in and out of rehabilitation centers. "We didn't accept 'Sly' in our therapy sessions," Dr. Richard Sapp reported to *Spin* magazine about the singer's stay in the Lee Mental Health Clinic in Ft. Myers, Florida. "Sylvester can control Sly. . . . Once he realized that we were serious, he became Sylvester. As long as he continues to do that, he shouldn't be having problems with drugs." Sly wasn't quite ready to control himself, though, and Serena-Marie Sanfilipo, a woman he'd met by chance in Florida, stepped in to help. She claims to have served as his court-assigned drug therapist, but her service seems to have been at times both intimate and unusual. "After I saw that people just kept giving him crack, I just locked him up in my house," she recounts in an interview. "I had to be with him for all the tours, and all the rehabs. . . . He kept having to go back into rehab."

Despite the drugs and the consequences, Sly made himself available to occasional musical collaborators during the '80s. They included George Clinton, Bobby Womack, and Jesse Johnson, the last a talented representative of the next generation of funk and a sometime colleague of emerging funk royalty Prince. Bobby took Sly under his wing during a spell in rehab in 1984. "We used to be as tight as bark on a tree," Bobby later lamented to the *Washington Post*. "As the drugs set in, the warm, creative side went away. And then it got worse and worse." Sly also worked on occasional tracks and demos, in the preceding and following decades, with REO

Speedwagon, Elvin Bishop, the New Riders of the Purple Sage, the Temptations, Bonnie Pointer, Gene Page, the Brothers Johnson, Maceo Parker, and Earth, Wind & Fire.

In November 1987, Sly was scheduled for two nights at the Las Palmas Theatre in L.A., where a *Los Angeles Times* reviewer found the sound system inadequate and Sly's voice "thin and strained when he tries to sing high melodies," perhaps a side effect of coke or uppers. Returning to the venue on the following night, Sly was arrested for allegedly owing $2,500 in back child support. The previous night's performance would count at his last real gig for almost twenty years.

Sly paid off his child-support debt the following month, but at some point prior to his scheduled preliminary hearing on drug charges in February 1988, he seems to have gone missing. It wasn't until November 14, 1989, that the watchful staff of the *Los Angeles Times* was able to report that Sly was being "held without bond in Connecticut pending extradition to California, where he is wanted on a 1987 drug-possession charge." The FBI informed the paper that "Stone has been living in Connecticut and New Jersey and has used the alias Sylvester Allen." Sly was returned to his home state and ordered to spend nine to fourteen months in a drug rehab center. Serena-Marie Sanfilipo, who'd tried to intervene in Florida years earlier, relocated to California to tend to Sly again. She took to parking outside his designated treatment center, to keep an eye on her charge. "He would mop the floor if someone else wouldn't mop it, so that people would like him," observes Serena. "He was an absolute perfect person in rehab. He did everything to make people happy [and] make people laugh. He played his keyboard. He was very joyful for other people, but he was just very lonely and sad. . . . He said, 'As much as I hate being here, it's better than being in jail.'" When she managed to get inside the center, "I would light a candle for him and we'd say a couple prayers and sing a couple songs, and he'd write music." After being discharged, "He was like a fawn," she remembers, "very fragile, having a tough time, but very happy." She says Sly then "cut ties with a lot of people that were negative," and that he invited her to move in with him. But she was put off by the threat of the return of bad habits. If Sly were ever turn over a new leaf, he would be the only one who could make himself stay away from the blow.

Sly grew ever more inaccessible to his biological family, including parents, siblings, and his three children. (Another daughter, Novena, had been born in the late '70s to Olenka Wallach of Sausalito, California.) "My brother's angry," Freddie told *Spin* in 1985, after withdrawing from his own cocaine habit. "He's been conned so many times, he's become a real con man himself." "I've cried into my pillow so many nights," added their mother, Alpha Stewart, "but I pray there's a God who can save Sly." Sly, in the same article, was dismissive of his connection with his own three offspring. "They do what they want," he stated. "I see them in and out."

Child-support bills, legal costs, and an estimated $3.4 million in back taxes, along with the disappearance of opportunities to record and perform, forced Sly to look for money. In September 1984, he sold his publishing interests to Mijac Music, owned by Michael Jackson, who was then on top of the music world (and a Sly admirer). Sly did manage to record several demos in the latter part of the '80s, some with fellow felon Billy Preston, but they weren't developed into moneymakers. For the 1987 movie *Soul Man*, Sly sang "Eek-A-Bo-Static" and a duet with Martha Davis of the Motels, "Love and Affection"; but neither charted.

Nostalgia-bound fans of the sounds of the Family Stone in the '60s and '70s might be tempted to assume that Sly's music would have faded in the '80s, even if its maker hadn't, due to changes in taste. Although the under-appreciation accorded Sly's post-band-breakup recordings of the '70s may have been due in part their being out of step with the dominant disco sound, it's likely that Sly, who was always ahead of his time, could have stayed on the charts if his mental and financial resources hadn't been detoured by drugs. One of his chief disciples, Prince, in fact did very well in the '80s. Like Sly, Prince was a black multi-instrumentalist, producer, songwriter, and arranger who had taken full control of his artistic output. Again like Sly, he attracted a significant white audience to his work, incorporating strains of hard rock and dance pop into his very personal brand of contemporary R & B. Both Prince and Sly had transcended the commercial and stylistic constraints of race, but the groundbreaking Sly had ended up struggling to hold on from day to day.

Early in the 1990s, Sly remained a shadow, even to his parents. His communication with them was spotty, but his mother, Alpha, insisted to *Mojo*, "I know he's a good man, God watches over him." "You can usually tell what he's been doing from the way he is on the phone," added papa K. C. "Mama knows the moment he says 'Hello' if she's talking to Sly or Sylvester. If he tries to tell a ten-minute story in ten seconds, then it's been a Sly Stone kinda day."

Jerry Goldstein took over management of Sly Stone in the early '90s. In a manner evocative of psychologist Eugene Landy's tough appropriation of care of the Beach Boys' fragile Brian Wilson in the 1970s and '80s, Jerry became Sly's guardian and personal supervisor, keeping inquisitive promoters, reporters, biographers, and ex-Family Stone members at bay. Jerry was a music veteran himself, having co-written the 1963 smash "My Boyfriend's Back" for the Angels, and later forming and performing in the Strangeloves, who recorded the first of many versions of the bubblegum standard "I Want Candy." Later he slipped behind the scenes to become a producer, and also served as manager for the great interracial funk act War. For better (Sly seemed to free himself from drugs for a while) or worse (Sly had no authority over his own catalog of compositions), Sly put his career, such as it was, in Jerry's charge.

GEORGE CLINTON INDUCTED SLY & the Family Stone into the Rock 'n' roll Hall of Fame in January 1993. Other legends ushered in that year included Sly contemporaries the Doors, Cream, and Creedence Clearwater Revival. While the original Family received their accolades, a quiet and withdrawn Sly, dressed as if he'd been taking fashion tips from Prince, came to the podium and made a very short thank-you speech, closing with, "See you soon." The players from his old band had not expected to see him there, and reaped little from his appearance. "When we were starting out," Jerry reminded *People* magazine, "Sly Stone had the power to control 80,000 people with his eyes. But in '93, he couldn't even look at me."

In 1995, Sly was back in rehab, spending forty-five days in the Brotman Medical Center in L.A. "He went in by choice, to concentrate on getting healthier," his son Sly Jr., then training to be a sound engineer, explained to *People*. "He's had problems because he hasn't been able to grow up. He's meant no harm to anyone." Sly remained rooted to the L.A. area through the '90s, though he was often in hot water with landlords and hotel managers. "In a sense, my father has wasted a lot of years," allowed Sly Jr. "But he's purposely stayed away from the spotlight and the pressure. He hasn't wanted attention."

But toward the end of the decade, there were healthy signs that Sly, or maybe Sylvester, was preparing himself properly for the new millennium. In 1997, he extended a rare summons to a young MIT graduate student named Jon Dakss, who'd established the slyfamstone.com Web site. Jon went to Los Angeles in April of that year to help Sly learn how to make use of his computer and the Web: "Though he assured me it was nothing personal," Jon related on his Web site, Sly "insisted on observing all that I did with his computer, and asked that I explain whatever I was going to do before I did it." Jon pronounced Sly to be in good spirits and in good health, living with a pair of sisters as aides. "They set up his equipment and perform on his songs. If Sly has lyrics, they write them down." For his trouble and devotion, Jon was given a spontaneous display by Sly on keyboards, to which he reacted, "I think he hasn't made a comeback because he doesn't want to. He could take the world by storm right now if he wanted to."

In 1998, Joel Selvin released *Sly & the Family Stone: An Oral History*. It presented a collection of interviews with Family Stone veterans, Stewart family members, and business and personal acquaintances of Sly, though the man himself did not share any thoughts with Joel. "Most of the people interviewed for this book have never spoken about their experiences before and many of the others have never publicly discussed some of these matters," ran Joel's introduction. "It's easy to understand their reluctance."

Alas, some of them became more reluctant after the publication of Joel's book. Jerry counted himself among the several people less than pleased with how they'd figured in Joel's handling of the story. Jerry stated to this author, in 2006, "I am not going to have any kind of negative comments to make about Sly & the Family Stone, because I've already been misquoted so much. . . . Everybody's been bit so much. So you are coming along at a time when I have scars on my heart." "That's the dirty laundry, the trash," said

Greg about Joel's book. "And that's not what [the group] was about, really."

In 1999, documentarians Nina Rosenblum and Dennis Watlington were engaged by New York Times Television to create a film about the careers of Sly and Jimi Hendrix, which took its title, *The Skin I'm In*, from one of *Fresh*'s lesser known but more soulful tracks. Reflecting on the project, director Nina allows that the view through her lens was rosier than that through Joel's glasses. "We really think that Sly Stone was a complete unadulterated genius . . . the likes of Rembrandt, Michelangelo, Mozart," she avows. As for Sly's diversion from artistic purpose, "He was like a reed, so in touch, as great artists are, with the times he lived in," says the filmmaker. "When things get repressive, [artists] really suffer, and I think he really suffered. The times went one way, and he went a different way. . . . Now, everything that that generation won is with us, in terms of civil rights and women's rights and understanding—the world will never be the same. But I think Sly paid for it. . . . He was taken away from us."

Among its many high points, the film, now available in the form of a director's rough cut, included footage shot at brother Freddie's Evangelist Temple Fellowship Center in his hometown of Vallejo, affiliated with the Church of God in Christ. His mother, Alpha, who had carried her family's connection to that denomination from her native Texas, spoke to the filmmakers from one of the temple's pews, bedecked in her Sunday finery, just a few years' before her and her husband K. C.'s passing. "Freddie came home [to Vallejo], and I was so glad," she testified. "I thought he might draw Sly. And maybe someday he will." She remembered that Sly, her older son, "just really was good in church . . . people would be hollering." Flashing forward, she commented, "I don't know what happened to him. It has to be the drugs." *The Skin I'm In* also featured input from music teacher David Froehlich, ex-manager David Kapralik, Bobby "The Swim" Freeman, and Billy Preston, as well as every member of the Family Stone except its leader. "The production company tried every which way [to reach Sly], but it wasn't to be," admits Nina. "We went to Beverly Hills, we tried to stake it out, we went to his front gate, we rang the bell—nothing. His family tried on our behalf, but it was difficult for them, too."

Dennis Watlington, the African American author and filmmaker who conducted most of the documentary's interviews, secured the Stewart family's input. "He came from the church, so when he showed up, they knew he was one of them, from them, by them, so we had much more access than we would ever have had," Nina points out. On camera, Jerry and Greg made reference to the deleterious effects of drugs, and record exec Steve Paley pointed out that Sly "loves being the Howard Hughes of his generation, he loves being inaccessible, he loves the idea that nobody knows who he is, where he is, or what he's doing and what his music is like. He loves being a legend." From a slightly different but equally amiable angle, George Clinton referred to his fellow performer and substance abuser as a "funny, witty, crazy, clever, half-ass would-be pimp," and noted that "he had to be what he was: father, preacher, he had the best of all the things they needed to do what they did." Billy Preston, interviewed in his kitchen, revealed, "It's always a dream, to get this long keyboard that we both play. If you ever see Sly," he told the filmmakers, pounding his chest and smiling, "tell him that I love him from the heart!" Billy passed away in 2006.

As aired on the Showtime cable television network, *The Skin I'm In* appeared in a version significantly edited by network functionaries, and was closer to the "sorry crawl" associated by Nina with Joel's oral history than to the sprightly, respectful time trot intended by her and Dennis. "When we gave it to Showtime, what we thought was one of the best things we had ever done got cut up into something else altogether, like a rag story from a tabloid," she laments. "It was really a cheapening of Sly: Sly the bad boy, Sly the drug addict, without really any human or social dimension. We were very, very, very shocked." So, yet again, were some of the interviewees. The filmmakers were put in the position of having to disseminate apologies and explanations, which were generally accepted, though the experience may have revived suspicions about interviews and media exposure. Sly himself has not registered any opinion about the Showtime documentary. About Joel's book and the print media in general, he proclaims, "I don't read all of that. I don't even know about Joel Selvin."

Keeping to his private music making, and far away from the public in an L.A. hillside home during the later '90s, Sly came to depend upon Mario Errico, the older brother of his former drummer Greg, as factotum and confidante. Mario, six years Greg's elder, got to know Sly while roaming San Francisco's North Beach nightlife in the mid-'60s. By the time the Family Stone, including Greg, had launched their performing career at Winchester Cathedral down the Peninsula, Mario was married and a father and thereby somewhat constrained in his night moves. Through several marriages, Mario held a variety of day jobs, while keeping contact with his brother and with Sly, and responding to occasional calls for help from the latter, until he became something of a live-in helpmate in L.A. "There's lots of times I inspire him to do certain things, and it works," says Mario, " 'cause he loves a lot of the things I love," including "music, motorcycles, and cars." The elder Errico was one of Sly's few acquaintances invited to extended stays in his abodes. Like many men in middle age, both Sly and Mario ultimately became restless to head down new roads in search of some of what had excited them long ago on the old ones.

As nostalgic pop music, by the turn of the twenty-first century, Sly & the Family Stone's oeuvre received ever-wider (and newly lucrative) exposure in TV shows, ads, and dozens of films. Crossover to the youngest generations was powered by the presence of the Family Stone on soundtracks of the popular *Shrek* movies, *A Knight's Tale*, and more recently the retro comedy *Semi-Pro*. Jerry reports that he and other band members have reaped particularly bountiful benefits from commercial mechanical royalties for repeated usage of their songs for selling Toyotas ("Everyday People") and Carnival Cruises ("Hot Fun in the Summertime"). With attribution but not compensation, pithy messages and catch phrases embedded within Sly's lyrics show up daily in media worldwide, even when the stories have nothing to do with music. Commenting on the problems and potential of humanity, Sly seems to have created his own gospel.

The band's irresistible integration of kaleidoscopic soul and get-down funk forged templates for pop, rock, rap, and hip-hop. Those in their creative debt, acknowledged or not, include the Beastie Boys, Living Color, Lenny Kravitz, and the Red Hot Chili Peppers, whose extravagantly thumpin'-and-pluckin' bassist Flea has borrowed Larry's bass brilliance. The Chili Peppers ably covered *Fresh*'s seductive "If You Want Me to Stay" in 1985, as did four-string luminary Victor Wooten on a live medley with "Thank You (Falettinme Be Mice Elf Agin)" in 2001. Hip-hoppers Arrested Development fashioned "People Everyday" as a sharp rewrite of "Everyday People," doubling the take with a bonus "Metamorphosis Mix" on their 1992 album. With the advent of digital, snippets of Sly & the Family Stone's songs seemed to emerge everywhere as backbeats, riffs, and fanfares on the tracks of Everlast, Too Short, De La Soul, Fatboy Slim, Janet Jackson, the Beastie Boys, Kid Rock, Ice Cube, Public Enemy, and others. The enduring influence of Sly extended even further. In the sophisticated and demanding arena of jazz, from which he'd long ago attracted the innovative Miles Davis, Sly became the co-subject of a seminar conducted at New York's Symphony Space in 2000 by irrepressible jazz clarinetist Don Byron, titled *Contrasting Brilliance: The Music of Henry Mancini and Sly Stone*. Several years later, "Stand" (with plenty of punch but no exclamation point) was extended to become the longest track, at eleven minutes, on trumpeter Wallace Roney's simply-titled album *Jazz*. And Jamie Davis sang a suave "If You Want Me to Stay" on his 2008 big-band album *Vibe Over Perfection*, produced and with drumming by Greg Errico.

In 2001, over the waves in Holland, a pair of thirty-something Dutch twins, Arno and Edwin Konings, embarked on a massive long-term project (still in process) to annotate every detail of every year of Sly's life and every track he'd ever recorded. Their research made them aware of the primarily sensationalist approach of most journalists and other writers to the subject of Sly, "especially how he wasted his life," says Edwin. "I was stunned," he continues. "Here was one of the greatest groups ever, in our opinion, and everything that people talk about is the not showing up, the drugs, and they don't talk about the greatness of the music."

The Rhythm and Blues Foundation presented Sly & the Family Stone with its Pioneer Award in 2001, for "lifelong contributions [which] have been instrumental in the development of rhythm and blues music." Sly didn't join his bandmates at the ceremony in Philadelphia.

I Love You for Who You Are

2002–

There should be someplace that we sit down
and say, "Hey, let's work it out, let's get on the
good foot together. Let's let bygones be
bygones."

—JAMES BROWN
1993 interview with Jeff Kaliss

I think my fans will follow me into our
combined old age. Real musicians and real fans
stay together for a long, long time.

—BONNIE RAITT

MOST OF THE ORIGINAL MEM-bers of the Family Stone con-vened in the back of a music store in Vallejo, California, in 2002, with the intention of recording again under the Family Stone name. Larry, who, with Greg, had been declared, in June of that year, one of the "25 Greatest Rhythm Sections of All Time" in *Drumming* magazine, expressed interest in a band reunion during the Rhythm and Blues Pioneer Award

induction, but neither he nor Sly showed up in Vallejo, and Rustee Allen took over the bass duties. Activity extended into 2003 and
to a studio in L.A., but Freddie declined to join a follow-up tour
and funding dried up. The project was dropped, but not before the
participants made a spirited appearance on funk scholar Rickey
Vincent's annual Sly birthday radio show on KPFA-FM in
Berkeley.

Eager to maintain momentum, Greg accepted an invitation
from a couple of local promoters to assemble a band for the San
Francisco Funk Festival in 2004. "We did it as the San Francisco
Funk All-Stars," he says. "I called Vet [Stewart] and Tiny [Mouton,
both from Little Sister], and I got Jerry and Cynthia, Fred Wesley
on trombone. . . . My intentions were just to bring the music, the
integrity and the spirit of it, on the stage. I wasn't trying to recre-
ate a Sly, that was the last thing I wanted to do." He hoped, though,
that the enterprise might, somehow, some time, tempt Sly to join
in. After the gig, at San Francisco's Great American Music Hall,
Greg summoned Jerry, Cynthia, Vet, and Tiny to team up with
bassist Bobby Vega and guitarist Gail Muldrow (both of whom had
played on *High on You*) and vocalists Skyler Jett and Fred Ross, in
a group called the Funk Family Affair. "I was getting offers, and I
saw it very clear in my mind what to do," says Greg. "But I found
myself wrestling with the understanding of what it was, what it
could be, and just trying to get it done."

The new group was booked for "Quiet Storm" radio station
KBLX's Stone Soul Picnic, on Memorial Day 2004 on the Cal State,
Hayward campus. For Greg, it was "a musical letdown. . . . We
went onstage and it just fell apart." Greg determined to form yet
another band, the Family Stone Experience, with singer Ian
Neville, son of the Neville Brothers' Aaron, from New Orleans, and
without Vet. Greg arranged for this band to showcase for booking

agents in Las Vegas, but soon began experiencing dissent among the players. "Some of the individuals in the band thought they should be making a fortune 'cause this was 'the Family Stone,'" Greg attests. "There was a lot of misconception of perspective of reality." Jerry, says Greg, specifically challenged him about leadership of the group. Ultimately, Greg "stepped out of the way. I went, if I'm gonna do this anymore, I'm gonna do it with the Man [i.e., Sly] himself . . . because you don't know how many times, over the last thirty years, people have come up to me and said, 'Well, c'mon, we'll kidnap Sly and bring him up to the country and put him in a studio and he'll want to do it.' I've heard every kind of story you could imagine, knowing none of them could ever work. And everybody's tried everything, from Clive Davis to Jerry Goldstein to who knows what."

Thus began the schism that resulted in the formation of two Family Stone spin-off bands: the Family Stone Experience, under Jerry's leadership, and the Phunk Phamily Affair, under Vet's. Greg went off, in 2005, to form Unity Music with producer Sam Beler and singer Jamie Davis, primarily devoted to showcasing Jamie's impressive, mellow chops in a big-band jazz setting. Meanwhile, the funky canon he'd helped create and had tried to resurrect started appearing on display stands alongside the lattes and Wi-Fi in Starbucks, under the title *Higher!*, a user-friendly compilation of Sly & the Family Stone hits, within the coffee giant's new Hear Music Opus collection of market-friendly CDs. Starbucks also marketed *Different Strokes by Different Folks*, a re-imagining of several Family Stone hits by young "urban" performers. These were apparent efforts to appeal both to older Sly fans and to their contemporary offspring. Vet's band got booked for an August 15, 2005, performance at L.A.'s Knitting Factory, a venue for jazz and "new" music, like the older club of the same name in New York.

Vet, who now lives in a comfortable house in a newer section of her native Vallejo, had been in touch with her older brother, who, she says, "was kind of moved that I would take this on, after all these years, doing all the old songs, as opposed to something new." She called Sly and asked him to transport her to the Knitting Factory and was surprised when he assented. No one had seen him in public for a long time.

"I didn't think I was going to hold him to it," she says. "So on the night of the gig, I went to his house [in Beverly Hills], and I said, 'The gig's in about an hour.' And he went down and said, 'Something's wrong with the bike.'" A sometime collector of cars old and new, luxurious and not, Sly had recently begun to accrue motorcycles. "I said, 'You just gotta flip that switch,'" Vet continues. "He forgot that he told me how to work the bike. So . . . he went upstairs and got dressed, I was dressed up, and he came down and said, 'We're gonna stop by Hollywood Boulevard.'

"So I'm on the back of his bike, and we go down and stop at this store called Zebra. We go into the store and he says, 'Dress my baby sister up, she's got a show to do! Dress her up like a biker!' And they did," Vet giggles. "I had on Harley-Davidson boots, the corset thing, the big baggy pants, the whole thing. . . . So I got back on the bike . . . and when we got there, they lifted up the side of the Knitting Factory so that Sly could drive his bike in. But Sly didn't drive right in, he sat outside, and people were just everywhere, and the tears were really flowing from people, because they really thought he'd died. People were just snapping pictures, and he was just as calm and collected as he could be." Sly was taken to a closed-off booth on the Knitting Factory's second level, while his sister joined the Phunk Phamily Affair onstage. "To me, that was one of the best shows we'd ever done," she says. "And when I looked up, where Sly was, I threw him a kiss, and he was dancing away. And I thought to myself, 'Dancing to his own music!' And after the show . . . he said to me, 'You know what, you guys play my music better than I've ever heard anyone play it in my life.' That's when he took a real interest in us."

And the wider music world seemed to be regenerating interest in Sly, or at least in what they remembered of him. Don Was, successful producer of acts as diverse as Iggy Pop, Bob Dylan, the Rolling Stones, Paula Abdul, and Waylon Jennings, positioned Sly & the Family Stone among "The Greatest Artists of All Time" in his 2004 article in *Rolling Stone*. Sly "is a singular folk orchestrator; Duke Ellington is probably the best reference point," Don declared, before choosing another laudatory comparison from the world of art. "As time went on, Sly started using some more dissonant colors; he became like the Cézanne of funk. It's like he took these traditional James Brown groove elements and started putting orange into the picture." Don went on to reflect on the era of his great artist's greatest hits. "The so-called revolution that was coming at the end of the Sixties: We might have lost that one, but Sly won his own personal revolution, musically and in the minds of the audience. I just hope he knows that, and maybe that he's OK with it. I hope he's not sitting around with any kind of remorse. Because by any real criteria that you could measure success, this guy is a titan."

A somewhat longer tribute to Sly and to a particular landmark album appeared in 2006 in the form of Paris-based African American pop culture critic Miles Marshall Lewis's brief but fascinating booklet *There's a Riot Goin' On*. Miles provided some interesting biographical info and a valuable, if questionable, perspective on the connections between Sly's music and hip-hop and between Sly's struggles and those of African Americans in general. Miles makes special mention of the influence of Sly's introduction of percussive "break beats" and of an attitude in lyrics that sounds "pretty hip-hop boastful, like LL Cool J."

Shortly into 2006, the National Academy of Recording Arts and Sciences issued a press release announcing that a special tribute to "legendary funk band" Sly & the Family Stone would take place at February's Grammy Awards ceremony at the Staples Center in Los Angeles. Guesting in the tribute would be a couple of veteran performers and a bunch of younger Grammy-nominated acts. No explanation was given of what any of the listed guests had to do with Sly and his band. But at the very least, it seemed, the Grammys would serve as an opportunity for yet another reunion of most of the members of the original Family Stone—and maybe for Sly's first public appearance since the Hall of Fame inductions thirteen years ago.

"There were lots of rehearsals," reports Jerry, "and Sly came to some of them, up in Hollywood. . . . [He] didn't participate too much. . . . He just listened. And I was really glad to see him. I said, 'I love you, man,' and he goes, 'I love you too, Jerry,' and I'll remember that always."

Another perspective on the rehearsal process, reported in the *Los Angeles Times*, described how Sly "came to a keyboard at center stage and made eye contact with no one. Still lean, but beneath the hood he seemed smaller than he was in the '60s. . . . His voice was robust and clear. . . . His left hand and wrist were in a cast" (variously attributed to a motorcycle spill and to a tumble on his hillside property). The executive producer of the upcoming telecast, John Cossette, seemed disappointed in Sly's demeanor, remarking, "He's not doing this, he's not hiding out for fifteen years to do what you just saw."

The show, on the evening of February 8, 2006, seemed something like an effort to usher rock 'n' roll itself past the age of retirement. Youthful luminaries like Mary J. Blige, Jay-Z, Alicia Keys, and Linkin Park heralded onstage performances at the Staples Center by an ageless Stevie Wonder and a more visibly weathered U2 and Paul McCartney. Unlike Sly, these were veterans who'd never strayed far from the spotlight and had maintained their careers across the decades.

The Family Stone tribute was delayed till well into the latter part of the telecast, no doubt keeping Sly fans worldwide wondering what would happen. Sly himself was later reported to have conveyed himself to the Staples on a motorcycle, and then to have been turned away by a security guard suspicious of his appearance. Finally comedian Dave Chappelle declared to the audience, "The only thing harder than leaving show business is coming back." The stage was then populated by a select showcase of newer rockers, including the Grammy-nominated band Maroon 5 and Will.I.Am of the Black Eyed Peas, as well as John Legend, Joss Stone, Devin Lima, and self-declared Sly disciple and slide guitar wizard Robert Randolph. The venerable Steven Tyler and Joe Perry of Aerosmith joined their juniors in launching a curious amalgamation of Sly & the Family Stone hits. If you looked hard, with little help from the show's director and cameramen, you could make out original Family Stone members Freddie, Rose, Cynthia, Jerry, and Greg, though not at the center of the stage. Larry, claiming illness, had been replaced at the last minute by Rustee Allen.

The multi-generational booking may have helped bridge the gap between older and younger fans, but the former were unlikely to have approved of the alterations they were hearing to well-remembered solid songs. Nor did they get much of the man who'd created that music, who was shouted-out by Steve Tyler, partway into "I Want to Take You Higher," Sly's mud-shaking hit at Woodstock: "Hey, Sly, let's do it like we used to do it!" Sly made his entrance from stage right, wearing a spacey outfit and topped by an adhesive blond Mohawk. He made a modicum of music and departed. It was by no stretch of the imagination a fair tribute to his value as creator, performer, and entertainer, and for many watching at the Staples and around the globe, it was something of a letdown. But the appearance somehow encapsulated much about the old Sly story: unpredictable, uncontrollable, and fantastic.

In the days that followed, the *Washington Post* referred to the "tentative and frail" appearance of "the J. D. Salinger of pop," and *Rolling Stone* wondered, "Where has Sly been? No one seems to know for sure. Will we ever see him again?" "Just the fact that Sly showed up that night, as busted up as he was, showed me he really wanted it to happen," added Aerosmith's Joe Perry, who knew something firsthand about the long-term consequences of coke. "I hope he got a taste of what it's like having the band behind him. Maybe that's the only thing that will get him going."

"It was fun, it was great, it was good," says Greg about the Grammys. But "there were a lot of things that could have been better. They should have given us the stage. . . . In some ways, I could say Sly shouldn't have come out, and if he did, he should have been prepared to do something and follow up right after." "Really, that wasn't my gig," Sly himself told *Vanity Fair*.

In retrospect, it seemed that the selection of the Grammy tribute band and the positioning of eight of the non-Family artists at the front of the Grammy stage may have been intended to promote the *Different Strokes by Different Folks* album, originally marketed by Starbucks and more recently reissued by Epic/Sony. All eight artists were involved in the album's remixes, and Jerry Goldstein was its executive producer.

"I don't think it was necessarily his platform—I thought it made stars of other people" is Vet Stone's perceptive comment about the tribute to her brother. "But all in all, I think [Sly's] only reason for being there, knowing him, could only be saying 'Thank you' to people who stood by him all these years: his fans. It was his way of saying, 'Thank you very much, I love you, and I will be back.'" With the help of his baby sister and some significant others, Sly soon began getting back to his public.

To help her brother reconnect with his roots and his public, Vet facilitated his relocation to Northern California. With her parents' passing, K. C. in 2001 and Alpha in 2003, her mission had been reinforced. "Before my mom and dad left, they told me, 'Go and get your brother,'" she shares. "And that's exactly what I did. . . . I went to L.A. and told him what Mom and Dad had told me, and he thought about it and said, 'Find me a house. I'm ready to come home.' It took me a while, but I found what he wanted." In 2006, Vet located a rentable property in the hills between Napa and Solano counties, a short drive from their childhood home and her own spacious modern residence in Vallejo. Compared to Sly's digs in L.A., the wine country mansion, formerly occupied by actress Sharon Stone (no relation), afforded "more privacy, it's larger, and it's got exactly what he wanted, like the pool, the guesthouses, and the garage space. He has space to put all of what I call his 'toys,' his bikes and things." The first time Vet was able to take Sly on a walk-through, he was entranced. "There's this lake at the side of the house, and he pointed to it and said, 'I could write a song right here.' And I thought, 'Whew, wow! That's how much he loves this house.' This is right. This is his home."

The year that opened with the Grammy homage continued to serve as one of reckoning for other Family members. A Family Stone spin-off band, captained by Jerry and including both Cynthia and Rose, appeared in October 2006 at the neon-skirted Cache Creek Casino resort, in California's Sacramento Valley. The three "originals" were ceremoniously brought onto the stage by the band's younger players, who included Bay Area–based singer Fred Ross. The casino club's audience was similarly multi-generational, from twenty-something officemates off on a weekend lark to retirement-age peers of the Family hoping to recoup some of their youth if not (at the slots and tables) their wagered pensions. It quickly became apparent that what was going down onstage was vital and accessible enough to bridge any gap.

Rose, petite and lovely in middle age, came on strong and vibrant to "Sing a Simple Song." Cynthia had gained a few pounds since her salad days, but had lost little of her insouciance or her trumpet's bright brass, paired with Jerry's feisty sax on "Stand!" and other numbers. The crowd was ready to put slot fatigue behind them and take to the floor by the time Cynthia summoned them to "Dance to the Music." With "Thank You (Falletinme Be Mice Elf Agin)" pulsing over it a short while later, the dance area was nearly full. The non-original musicians were easily integrated into the band and the music, with vocalist Fred voicing his gratitude for being allowed to keep company with the trio of Family Stone veterans. Fred wore a white space cowboy getup, evocative of Sly's fringed duds at the 1969 Woodstock Festival. Tall and affable in celebrating, on that night, five years of marriage to his Bay Area wife, Rebecca, Fred assumed both Sly's lead vocals and Larry Graham's lower-pitched phrases. Additional singing came from Freddie Stone stand-in Vernon "Ice" Black, a showy but able lead guitarist, and from lead keyboardist Tache, aka Thomas Cryer. Blaise Sison slapped electric bass but didn't sing, and drummer John Mader, keeping to tradition, was the first and last instrumentalist heard from. It was a show traveling on nostalgia, but very much fueled by its own integrity and enthusiasm. Whether the full Family Stone itself would ever again take to a stage in that same spirit remained to be seen.

SLY MAY HAVE LONG AGO left the regular religious practice of his childhood, but it's not clear that religion ever totally left him. Rustee Allen recounted to Joel Selvin how Sly had once told him, "I've done so many shitty things, God's not gonna take me in now." But several of Sly's siblings have been ready to take him back to the faith.

The Evangelist Temple of the Church of God in Christ rests on a sunny corner of a large thoroughfare paralleling Route 80 on the western edge of Vallejo, not far from where K. C. and Alpha Stewart raised their tuneful offspring a half-century ago. The second-born son, Frederick J. Stewart, aka Freddie Stone, came into the new millennium as pastor of the temple, and his youngest and closest-living sister, Vaetta, aka Vet Stone, is a regular congregant. At her house, among the newer, tonier developments on the northeast corner of Vallejo, Vet explores what she sees as the uniformly positive effects of growing up in a Christian household. "My siblings are Christians, and as a Christian you can't harbor anger and hate, confusion and things, and remain a Christian," she testifies. "We were raised so that if there were a difference, we would go to each other and resolve it. We kept communication open, and that's still going on, let me make that very clear."

Vet also points out that she hears many of her brother Sly's lyrics as congruent with the family faith. "As a matter of fact, the lyrics to 'Everyday People,' they're being sung, as we sit here, on BET [Black Entertainment Television] and many gospel stations. They sing the identical lyrics Sly wrote. And I'm sure when Sly wrote that, he wasn't thinking that the gospel stations were gonna pick it up. But I could be sitting here on Sunday, looking at *Bobby Jones Gospel* [on BET], and here comes this group, very young, singing 'Everyday People,' and I think, 'Is this fantastic or what?' " Vet herself had come to the Family Stone to do background vocals,

155

forty years ago, directly from singing with the Ephesians Church of God in Christ, in Berkeley. Her family faith also deserves credit, Vet believes, for maintaining her eldest brother through his times of trouble, regardless of his responsibility for bringing the trouble on himself and whether or not he himself acknowledged divine intervention on his behalf. "I believe that God has had His hand on my brother's life through his whole life, as well as He has it now," she says. "I believe that my brother's life has been completely protected, and through the prayers of my mom and dad, God honored that. And I know that my mom and dad prayed for Sly, so for that reason I don't believe there's anything I could have done [for Sly] better than God." What she did do, of course, is to facilitate Sly's return to Northern California. Her mother, Alpha, would have been happy to know that although Sly is not a frequenter of his brother's church, as Vet is and she herself was, he's now at least within a short drive of what might remind him of how musical and joyful communal worship can be.

THE EVANGELIST TEMPLE is a joyful place for the curious to visit, as this writer did at Vet's invitation, on a sunny Sunday morning in the fall of 2006. The man credited by his peers as an enduring icon to aspiring lead guitarists now looks the part of a church elder, balding and wearing glasses, but his preparation for his church's weekly celebration is uniquely evocative of his former lifestyle. He straps an electric guitar over the robes of his office, and is fitted with a headset by his daughter, Joy, a lovely reflection of her mother, Melody, who sits attentively in her pew. On the wall behind Freddie (officially Pastor Frederick J. Stewart) are posted the four sections of the service—Prayer, Praise, Worship, and Power—and the week's gospel readings associated with each. Vet arrives in a tailored but lively dress, and the female portion of the gathering

African American congregation is, like Vet, arrayed in Sunday best, many of the older women also wearing generously decorated hats. While conversation burbles in the pews, the sounds at the front of the church resemble a run-up to a gig, with burps from Freddie's guitar and paradiddles from a young man on drums. Ready to provide keyboard support are Joy on a Kurzweil and Vet on a Hammond B-3, the instrument of choice of her eldest brother, Sly.

Reliably on time at the noon start of the service, Freddie announces, "Make a joyful noise unto the Lord! Whatever we need, we thank you for it. Whatever we don't need, we thank you for taking it away." It seems to summarize how, over a long life, he's gotten to where he is. Through the rest of the service, ritual worship and readings are interspersed with musical offerings, and both prove more enjoyable and inspiring than your average religious experience. "Where would we be if we had not let women go forth in the church?" asks the pastor at one point, then repeating the rhetorical question. Melody's response from her pew provokes general laughter: "Alone!" Referring to the Book of Joshua, and probably to the former fruits of his fame, Freddie declares, "We don't define success by money. Do you put your money ahead of your relations with your fellow man?" Several women in the congregation mutter softly but audibly, "Uh-huh." The pastor responds, "Y'all be jokin', but the Lord's gonna hear your joke! I'm talkin' about where you're supposed to go, now let's talk about where ya' go."

For the vocal musical numbers, the lyrics are projected on a screen with the expectation that the congregation will join in, at least on the choruses. There are good voices among them, sometimes recalling the uplift of the Edwin Hawkins Singers, who had themselves been based in their church, in Oakland, and had crossed over to the pop charts in the late '60s with "Oh Happy Day," alongside the Family Stone. Freddie affords himself a few soulful solo-guitar breaks, showing he still has what it takes, and his wife supplements the drums with raps on her tambourine. Vet and Joy remind the listener of how Sly made use of keyboards to get the thrill of gospel music onto some of his tracks.

Freddie knows how to keep up with his congregants' concerns with current affairs, and how to appeal to the younger churchgoers, including several of his own grandchildren. He preaches about the devil lurking behind ongoing racial divides, and about how much things have changed since he was a young player. "I can't go to those [hip] places any more," he says, bending over in mimed antiquity. "I'm just an old country preacher, preachin' the Gospel." Commenting more seriously on the lessons he's learned about detours from the Kingdom of Heaven, he points out, "All you have to do to get the Kingdom of the World is to be willing to lose your dignity and be degraded." He reminds his listeners, "My salvation is bigger than your not liking me, bigger than your not liking the way I sing or play the guitar." It's apparent, of course, that these people, who count themselves as family and friends, feel that they like him and his God-given musical talent very much. Following outreach with the collection plate and the sobriety of communion, the pastor rewards the congregation with a short scat, very much evoking the kind of jive lyrics he used to share with his sibling Sly: "When you know that you know that you know that you know that you know, amen, you can do it."

SLY'S RELOCATION FROM THE hyper heat of the L.A. hills to the bucolic, breezy heights of Napa County put him closer not only to his brother and one of his sisters but also to two of his offspring in the Sacramento area, son, Sly Stewart Jr., and daughter, Sylvette Phunne Robinson. He was also in close reach, when and if he decided to extend it, of three other members of the Family Stone: Greg in Petaluma, Jerry in Folsom, and Cynthia in Sacramento. "He wanted to come back up here where his group started—that was the idea, man," says Mario Errico, who made the move back to his native Bay Area alongside Sly and continued to function as Sly's right-hand man. Now somewhat frail and inclined to nervous energy, Mario approved of the "peacefulness" of the new Napa home, and the exercise gear that came with the rented mansion. Despite the tolls that hard living and middle age have taken on both men, "If he sees me get into [an exercise program], he'll do it, he'll follow," assures Mario. But most of Sly's days, at whatever hour they commence, are filled with "music, man. We take a little ride to the store, for groceries, clothes and things. Then back to the house. . . . He's got this Korg [keyboard], it cost about ten-and-a-half thousand. . . . He stays there, man, he loves it. . . . I'm down in the garage, messing around."

In tune with Mario's affections for Sly and wheeled vehicles, and standing high in Sly's confidence, is Neal Austinson. Twenty years younger than Sly and Mario, Neal grew up in Marin County and became a focused fan of the Family Stone while in high school. Through one of his schoolmates, a daughter of Jerry Martini, Neal got to visit Sly's pad in Novato while the marriage to Kathy Silva was still in place, though he got little one-on-one attention from Sly at that time. There were occasional interchanges during the '80s and '90s as Neal pursued his father's career in surveying, and in his off-hours began accumulating what is arguably the world's most complete collection of Sly & the Family Stone memorabilia and material. The Neal Austinson Archives include photographs, promotional papers, clothing, and audio and video recordings.

Now living in Santa Rosa, in Sonoma County, north of Marin, Neal found himself summoned by Sly for a variety of pragmatic and fanciful purposes, after Sly moved to Napa County, an hour's drive to the east. Neal's assignments ranged from registering vehicles to evaluating business opportunities (Sly briefly considered opening a rib house) to fielding requests from curious press and documentarians. "I would never violate Sly's privacy or do anything weird like that," he says. "I just feel extremely fortunate that I can pretty much go there any time I want. Nobody [else] really goes up there. From what Mario tells me, [Sly] likes me and trusts me. . . . It hasn't gotten to the point yet where he's let me hear anything, but he's let me read lyrics, and he's recited lyrics to me, too. I think he wants to share things with people, but he hasn't brought it to that level yet." Through the latter part of 2006, both Mario Errico and Austinson had taken steps to help me realize the hope that Sly would grant some personal experience to include in this book. "He's liable to," Mario remarked mysteriously over a December lunch. "You just gotta catch him at the right time."

Forty years after the formation of the Family Stone and thirty-five since the start of its dissolution, it looked like the band's founder was still making music—and still doing drugs. There had been little or no press coverage of either activity for a long time, though intimates reported that the latter had diminished as Sly had moved further from the fast lane. The other scattered remainders of the legendary band had been finding their way through middle age as best they could. Brother Freddie, long cleansed of his own drug problems, continued tending to his family, including several grandchildren, and to his flock at the Evangelist Temple Fellowship Center in Vallejo, where he presided every Sunday. Sister Rose began work on a book and a funky solo album (released in 2008 as *Already Motivated*). She also sang with Jerry Martini's group, while her daughter, Lisa, prepared to stand in for her in Vet's and Sly's various aggregations. Cynthia, living modestly in Sacramento, brightened all of the spin-off bands with her horn and spunky stage presence. Jerry helped form and lead several of those bands, catering to an abiding appetite for the sounds of the Family Stone by touring fairs, boardwalks, and the like. He also wielded his sax at local engagements in the greater Sacramento area while co-parenting a teenage daughter. Greg, raising a young family in Sonoma County, remained in demand for Bay Area all-star jams, but his principal focus was producing a couple of class-act big-band albums for vocalist Jamie Davis and getting Jamie out to a world whose nostalgia extended further back than the '60s. Larry, geographically and socially the most distant from his old mates, settled in Minnesota, close to the funky, unstoppable Prince, and sharing his devout Jehovah's Witness faith and some of his gigs.

ON NEW YEAR'S EVE, Neal relayed to me a phone call from Sly, summoning us to his place. Under entreaty from Neal, Sly rescheduled the meeting for New Year's Day 2007. At about eight the next morning, I left my San Francisco home (a mile north of the Urbano Drive site of the Family Stone's inception) and drove across the Golden Gate Bridge to rendezvous with Neal in Santa Rosa. But there was no reaching the habitually nocturnal Sly by phone at that early hour, so I spent several more hours lunching, chatting, and plotting with Neal what questions, of the many that had occurred to me, I could and should put to my elusive subject. Neal was well acquainted with Sly's taboos and defenses.

Late in the afternoon, after several phoned attempts, Neal and I determined to trust dumb luck and drive over to Sly's environs. The trip took us across the Napa-Sonoma Marshes Wildlife Area, lovely and tranquil, a contrast to Neal's obvious excitement. The air was crisp and cool, and the conversation, mostly about Sly, amusing. My guide picked a staging area, just off the freeway and within striking distance of Sly, to try phoning him again. After several tries, his hope seemed to fade somewhat, but around 3 p.m. he reached Phunne, Sly's daughter with Cynthia, who was visiting. She told Neal that her dad had been up late the previous night, not ushering in 2007 but working on his music, and that he was still asleep. A while later, she confirmed his rising and gave us the green light.

Neal navigated me along the rural road leading the way up among the hills to the pretty place Vet had found for her brother, well hidden from the hoi polloi and the media. A driveway off the road wound past oak trees toward a massive six-bedroom mansion, along a curved fence embracing the elongated, well-cultivated furrowed rows of a vineyard. Mario had referred to the grapes in a tale he'd shared with me about a recent visit by the landlords. "I made a joke with 'em, 'If Sly buys this place from you guys, the vineyards are going, man.' They go, 'Whaddya mean?' I go, 'We're gonna put thoroughbreds in there, man.' They didn't know what to say." Sly had no intention of becoming a vintner.

I was instructed by Neal to wait in the spacious garage while he ascended into the living quarters to announce me. I wondered if arrangements for a papal audience might be like this. It was a good time to take a look around at some of the "toys" for which Mario and Neal shared the responsibilities of registration and maintenance. They included a Hummer, a motorized scooter, and several massive brightly painted three-wheeled motorcycles, like the one with which Sly had gifted Vet. I'd seen it parked outside her home in Vallejo. On the walls of the open garage, above an enviable assembly of parts and tools, was a poster of Al Pacino in *Scarface* and the words *Money, Power, Respect*. The green, spicy aromatics of the outdoors overpowered any motor oil fumes.

A tall, attractive woman approached and introduced herself as Phunne. We chatted about how grateful she feels about seeing her father settled in such a benign environment, and how brisk it might get, so much cooler than the Hollywood Hills, should the wind blow over the vineyards later in the evening. Coming back down the stairs, Neal reported somewhat regretfully that Sly would prefer to prepare his own answers to a written list of questions, and have me return, later in the cool evening, to retrieve the list. I told Neal to tell Sly I'd already put in enough waiting and would prefer some action. After another unseen deliberation in the bowels of the mansion, Neal, in a brighter mood, said Sly would speak with me, but only for twenty minutes and without any recording device. I was given the impression that the ban on taping had been imposed by the ominous and unreachable manager Jerry Goldstein.

Clutching a notebook, I ascended the staircase into what looked to be the kitchen. I saw a slight, older man seated at the kitchen table, wearing casual clothes and a knit cap. He regarded me with a bemused expression, and I smiled back. But I kept looking past him, looking for the person I was expecting to encounter. Then Neal stepped up to introduce me to the seated man: "Sly, this is Jeff Kaliss; Jeff, this is Sly." I realized my mental image had been out of date.

Colleagues of mine and associates of Sly had warned me that he'd be expected to come across as confrontational, unresponsive, or unintelligible in interchange. But it had been twenty-one years since Sly's last in-person interview, and I had never been one to let my curiosity or my professionalism be compromised by my subjects' quirky reputations. My starting point for interviews has always been that I can have a friendly and informative conversation with anyone. I shook Sly's large hand, we exchanged New

Year's greetings, and I sat down, ready to scribble. Neal joined us at the table.

I knew Sly had recently given his sister Vet permission to call her band "The Family Stone," that this group had landed a gig in Anaheim, California, and that it was rumored that Sly might join in the performance. I told Sly that I'd be using my interview with him for a newspaper article in advance of Vet's show, as well as for a much bigger project, a book on Sly & the Family Stone. I asked him what he judged to be the most important element in telling such a story.

"The truth," he replied.

I got him to expand on the truth about what he'd been up to, up there among the grapevines. "I've been writing new songs," he said, "some on tape, some on paper, and some on tape and paper." What would he do with the new material? "I'll release them, with members of my family . . . my daughter [I assumed he meant Phunne], maybe my son, my nieces, and a grand-niece." For the news story, I felt it necessary to ask Sly what he thought about his sister Vet's ensemble, which I hadn't yet heard. "One of the best things is that they're all willing to do what it takes," Sly replied diplomatically. But are they willing to do it right? I wondered. "That's the main thing: they do it perfect."

Vet had said her group might release a debut album on Sly's PhattaDatta label, but it hadn't happened. Sly told me he'd have his own record of new material out by the end of the year, and that the prospect of returning to recording and performing helped him feel "new again." I asked him to say more about what might be on his new album. "Before, my songs had a lot to do with dealing with unnecessary fighting," he said. "And that's still the case." He quoted a fraction of one new lyric: *When you wind up / Making your mind up / That's when you'll find up / Instead of down.*" He was reciting instead of singing, but I had to tell him how wonderful it was to hear that rich basso voice up close. He smiled. Had coming back north brought him closer to his family, as Vet had hoped? "I see a lot of them," said Sly, "and they always have music on their mind. It takes more of the time than conversation." He reminded me, gently, that our talk would have to come to an end, because he wanted to spend more time with Phunne.

What about the way in which the public will view him, now that he's been so long out of the public eye? "I hope it's still that I'm doing music, and still representative of the truth." Would he be likely to let his long-waiting fans see him down in Anaheim later that month? "I feel like I'm gonna," he answered, shining that perennial beacon of a grin.

Driving back to Santa Rosa, Neal was bountifully pleased, and relieved. After I'd dropped him off and was headed south toward a delayed dinner, I got a call on my cell from Neal. He'd followed up by phone with Sly, who had complimented him on his judgment of character. Sly, it seemed, was happy with his brief return to being interviewed, and with the interviewer.

The resulting profile of Sly appeared in the *Los Angeles Times* on January 9. A couple of days later, Neal and Mario conveyed Sly and his live-in girlfriend, Shay, down the coast to Anaheim in a costly rented motor home, in which Sly was able to continue to work out on a keyboard. Despite the *Times* story, his imminence was to be kept secret from his fans till the last minute. I made my own way to Anaheim, curious about how Sly would do it, almost two decades since his last foreshortened gig at the Las Palmas in L. A.

At the House of Blues, adjacent to Disneyland in Anaheim, a sizeable crowd was kept waiting an hour and a half on the evening of January 13 for the start of what had been billed as the Family Stone show. Just like old times. "They're very patient," Dawn

Elder-D'Agostino, a regular at the venue, remarked to me. "If it was a punk crowd, they'd be raving." She added, "You don't see many crowds that are this diverse," in reference to the multiethnic, multigenerational audience. There were younger neo-hippies and designer-leather-jacketed Hollywood cognoscenti, but also a large portion of pre-punk Baby Boomers, happy to groove during their wait to a succession of funky songs played over the house system. Also in the throng were the twins Arno and Edwin Konings, who'd rewarded themselves for their continuing research on Sly by flying in from Holland, just for the concert. Positioned right up against the stage was a wise-looking lady in a wheelchair, sporting a flower in her graying hair. She was Serena-Marie Diflipo, Sly's one-time drug counselor and long-time informal advisor. They were all listening to the recorded sounds coming over the house system, of those funkmeisters who'd preceded Sly ("Sex Machine," James Brown), his contemporaries ("Atomic Dog," George Clinton; "Got to Give It Up," Marvin Gaye), and a few of the many he'd influenced ("Nasty Girl," Prince with Vanity; "Jungle Boogie," Kool & the Gang). Sometime around ten o'clock, the revelers were advised to "Put your hands together for Sly & the Family Stone." This heralded, to the sound of "Dance to the Music," the appearances of Vet, dressed in a three-quarter-length white jacket and gold boots, Skyler Jett, the designated male vocalist, wearing a leather jacket and leather pants, and Lisa Stone, Rose's daughter and Sly's niece, looking slim and lovely in an airy outfit. Cynthia, the only player lateraling between Jerry's and Vet's bands, also took the stage with three other horn players, one of them Pat Rizzo, who'd partnered with and then replaced Jerry in the original group. Four string and rhythm players completed Vet's lineup. But there was no sign of her celebrated sibling, and not even any confirmation of his proximity. Yet.

Through a string of nine tunes from the original Sly & the Family Stone songbook and a couple from Vet's lither days with Little Sister, Skyler acted as a sort of barker to the crowd, demanding, "How many people know this song?" and "How many people got Sly Stone records out there?" Skyler also mimicked the chuckle from the closing bars of "Sing a Simple Song," an odd affectation, since Sly's original chuckle had been an act of unrehearsed spontaneity (a reaction to Larry's apparently improvised lyric, "livin', lovin', overdubbin'"), and was not meant to be reproduced. In other aspects, the arrangements of this new Family Stone seemed intent on retrofitting the classic hits with the trappings of neo-soul and jazz. It was fun, however, and well-received by the assembled.

After the eleventh number, "Everybody Is a Star," Skyler reminded everybody that "this is a historical night, y'all!" And then the real star himself finally shuffled out onto the stage, and displayed a credible reaction to the rapt crowd. "I don't know whether any of you are as old as I am," Sly told them. He'd reattached his blond Mohawk, last seen at the Grammys, and had donned a military jacket with cape and red scarf. Sunglasses obscured his lustrous large eyes.

Over the next couple of songs, a couple of his daughters seemed bent on reinforcing him in curious musical forms: Novena was petite and cutely garbed and noodled some Chopin on one of the Yamaha Motif keyboards. Phunne, cool and long of limb, took the mike and rapped about family, while Sly laid down some keyboard funk behind her. Niece Lisa Stone helped make the event a literal Family Affair. Shay, who'd started with her sister as helpmates to Sly and became his regular female companion in Napa, joined the jam on an African drum.

Wandering to the front of the stage, Sly was greeted with cheers and camera flashes by the adoring throng. Responding with visible delight, he attempted to lead them in an aptly timed "Thank You (Falletinme Be Mice Elf Agin)," and no one seemed to mind that Sly had started the tune off in the wrong key. Grinning almost shyly, Sly was led by Mario offstage, where Neal and his lady, Jeanine, were waiting with congratulations. The formerly patient audience now chanted "We want Sly!" repeatedly. "He'll be back," promised Phunne. Vet, who'd been looking less than comfortable through much of the waiting for Sly, now seemed inspired by her brother's act of commitment, and she began some uptempo gospel sounds, suggestive of her time with the Heavenly Tones. Sly then returned to the stage to lead the house through the chanting portion of "I Want to Take You Higher," as he'd done for hundreds of thousands at Woodstock more than thirty-seven years earlier. Then he was gone again.

In a nice touch, Vet finished off the extended evening by acknowledging the upcoming Martin Luther King Day holiday and performing "Don't Call Me Nigger, Whitey." She and the band then covered "Sex Machine," which she dedicated "in honor of the great godfather of soul, James Brown," who'd passed away on Christmas morning.

The Konings twins from Holland later gifted Sly at his hotel with a vintage drum machine, like the one he'd deployed on *Riot*. This scored them some video ops for an accompanying Dutch TV crew. Sly was delighted, as he ought to have been. More than on the HOB stage, he was being treated like the esteemed elder of a vibrant tribe.

Through the rest of 2007, Sly's performances with Vet's reconfigured Family Stone band followed much the same suit as the year's opening gig, There was variation, though, in the degree and quality of Sly's participation and in the reactions of the everskeptical but always curious press and public. For a gig arranged by comedian/impresario George Wallace at the Flamingo in Las Vegas and scheduled for March 31, local bookmakers were betting forty-five to one that Sly wouldn't show. He beat the odds, taking to the stage after the band's introductory medley in what the *Las Vegas Sun* described as "a black sequined suit with black platform shoes and red heels, a red sequined shirt, a black belt with a giant rectangular plate reading 'Sly,' a black stocking cap, a neck brace, and big white Dolce & Gabbana shades." The outfit was enough to ignite '70s flashbacks in the "amped-up fans," even if Sly's half-hour performance was far short of what they recalled of those times (though still far longer than at the Grammys). The *Las Vegas Review-Journal* described Sly as "the ghost of R & B's past, a funk forebear who's finally come out of hiding." He made his way onstage with a pump of his fist, "looking like a perspiring gemstone, like he'd been covered in an imploded disco ball." The media differed in their assessments of Sly's voice and the band's coordination with him, but they lauded his interaction with the crowd. Sly "appeared to enjoy himself and regain his old funk form," reported the *PR Newswire*. "His smile was infectious, he slapped high fives with an adoring audience, and he even gave autographs as he walked amongst the fans. . . . He seemed particularly happy to introduce his daughters, Baby [Novena], a classical pianist, and Phume [Phunne], a rapper, as each of them shined in solo moments from the stage they were sharing with their dad during this eventful evening." Audience member and Family Stone ex-manager Ken Roberts, when questioned about Sly's brace, connected it to what he said was a large growth on Sly's spine. But Mario and others referred instead to a prolonged recovery from Sly's accidental tumble from a slope near his former Beverly Hills abode. Numerous amateur videos of the Flamingo show and later performances remain available on the Web.

A much anticipated box set of the seven Epic albums under the Sly & the Family Stone name was released in April 2007 as *The Collection*, in limited numbers, by CBS's Epic/Legacy division, complete with bonus alternate or unreleased tracks and both original and redacted liner notes by various rock writers. The most thorough presentation of Sly's work since Jerry Goldstein's admirable *The Essential* double album in 2002, the package inspired a new, almost universally laudatory cascade of reviews in the media and further nostalgia and anticipation among listeners. However, Sly, Vet, and Sly's lawyer, Greg Yates, cast doubt in interviews with *Vanity Fair* on Sly's connections with the box release and on Jerry Goldstein's management of the material and the finances. "As far as I'm concerned, there is no deal with [Jerry]," said Vet, and Greg added, "I've been retained by Sly Stone to represent him regarding issues surrounding contracts with other third parties for his publishing rights. . . . We are concerned about certain matters that he was kept in the dark about." In the same periodical, Clive Davis, who'd captained CBS and Epic during most of the launches of those albums, commented, "I have great regrets that it's taken Sly all these years to return, but the fact that there might be a happy ending to all this is a great feeling."

The *Vanity Fair* article was written by contributing editor and superfan David Kamp, who had "spent a dozen years chasing the former Sly & the Family Stone front man" and managed, with the help of Vet, to get an interview with Sly in the spring of 2007. The piece got global exposure but provided little new insight. "I get the sense," David wrote tellingly, "that Sly relishes this sort of opaqueness, letting people in just enough to intrigue and confound them."

Rumors had been circulating about a summer tour with Vet's band through Europe. An Independence Day weekend event in

San Jose, a couple of hours south of Sly's Napa base, gave him and Vet a chance to ramp up for the European junket. There were serious delays during the festival, dubbed "Back in the Day," but none due to Sly, and the eager anticipation of the featured act seemed not to diminish. Attended backstage again by Mario Errico and Neal Austinson, and ushered onto the outdoor stage by a very tall bodyguard of recent hire, Sly got to perform for only about fifteen minutes, dressed in a rather unbecoming bulky white hoodie, baggy jeans, baseball cap, and shades. Local police, mindful of permit restrictions, brought the proceedings to what both artists and audience considered a premature halt. The Bay Area press, having wondered whether their hometown boy might somehow make good, reacted with disappointment. The *San Jose Mercury-News*'s Shay Quillen credited Sly as "the most soulful person on stage," but berated Vet's Family Stone for not bringing him out until after several of his familiar hits and a couple of his creations for Little Sister had been played without him. Joel Selvin, there for the *San Francisco Chronicle*, praised the band's "extraordinary showmanship," but he noted that they "seemed more like a tribute band than a new model of the old standard," and that Sly's own voice was "hardly audible."

The tour abroad, for which the same basic ensemble took to the skies a few days later, also drew mixed notices. A reviewer in England's *Observer* seemed unaware of the history of Vet's band when he attended a performance in Italy and wrote, "It is somehow typical of Sly that he finally chooses to return without most of the original musicians who were such an integral part of the musical revolution he set in motion. In Perugia, they were sorely missed." A Swiss reporter caught the Family Stone's appearance at the Montreux Jazz Festival on July 14, and shared the *Observer*'s impression of Sly as "tired." The band itself was judged "very average." At the Blue Note Records Festival in Belgium, some spectators were said to be annoyed and to have demanded ticket refunds after a delayed and foreshortened performance. A TV5-Monde reviewer in Nice, France, told of "a weird and deceitful evening which didn't lift the veil of mystery surrounding this tortured personality." At the Pori Jazz Festival in Finland, Sly's "old and worn out voice" was bemoaned, as was the Family Stone's "correct and safe" delivery of the classic repertoire.

The very different scene at the venerable Olympia in Paris elicited memories of Sly's last visit there, twenty-seven years before, and drew praise from the city's *Funk-U* magazine. "I had arrived at the venue expecting nothing," wrote the reviewer, who took notice of Vet's familiar onstage angst, "looking for a sign of the roadies or sound engineer to know if her beloved brother would finally take her off the hook and finally appear." When Sly did show up to sing "If You Want Me to Stay," the writer determined that "the voice was there, almost unchanged after all these years." Even the trademark basso dip, delivering, *The kind of person / That you really are now*, had been preserved. The review went on to confirm that Sly, "looking at first pretty weak . . . got increasingly confident, thanks perhaps to the unbelievable and immediate response from the audience, which screamed all the lyrics." Sly even leapt off the stage to shake hands with the delighted front row. "You get some, you give some back," he later pronounced from the mike, before tossing his necklace and jacket as relics to the crowd.

In retrospect, the Olympia show stands out as the high point of the European tour. "When I saw him connect to the music again, that was really a joyful moment for me," commented Greg Errico, after watching video segments from the show on the Internet. "And I told him that, last night, on the phone," Greg continued.

"And he immediately knew what I was talking about: he said, 'That was the night!' I saw him jumping up, dancing, connecting with the music, connecting with the people, connecting with himself, connecting again. . . . He goes, 'I can't believe how rusty I was,' and I start laughing. I go, 'Sly, look at all the ball players. We're lucky, we have extended life expectancies, as musicians. Ball players are done when they're thirty. We're sixty! And you know what, you can still do it. But you gotta get out there.'"

It was encouraging, but also a little sad to see Sly retracing the steps of his formerly compelling tours without reaching the assured measure of magic that he and his fans still hoped for. But the reaction of the press and the public had to be assessed within the context of its own inherent foibles, as well as Sly's. On the dark side of America's obsession with fame is the envy that accompanies the admiration of celebrities, and which seems to feed directly into the joy of watching them crumble.

Two days before Thanksgiving 2007, and a couple of weeks later, Sly was happy to make it back onstage in New York City for the first time in thirty-two years, at B. B. King Blues Club and Grill on 42nd Street. The gigs had originally been promoted as a reunion of the Family Stone, but had to be recast after it was revealed that Freddie, Rose, Greg and Larry would, for a variety of reasons, not be playing. Dressed in a white sweat suit trimmed in silver, with sunglasses and Mohawk back in place, Sly was joined this time by two of his most stalwart Family Stoners, Cynthia and Jerry, as well as by Rose's singing daughter, Lisa, and the ensemble from the European tour minus Vet and Skyler. The *New York Times* reported, "He did sing, sporadically, and quite well, using something close to the eerie, insinuative voice that can be heard on *There's a Riot Goin' On*." The reviewer (and many others who witnessed him that year) felt particularly touched by Sly's "slithery" invocation of "If You Want Me to Stay," "which sounded more bittersweet than ever: *Count the days I'm gone / Forget reaching me by phone / Because I promise I'll be gone for a while.*" During "Sing a Simple Song," Sly excused himself from the stage, saying he had to urinate, an urgency he'd expressed frequently on recent tours. Rumor had it that this was code for a drug break, but Neal Austinson, serving as road manager in New York, says that in truth Sly was seeking time to go stretch out in his dressing room, to regain his stamina. He did indeed seem shaky on both entrances and exits, in New York and elsewhere. And his apparent physical vulnerability, along with sometime uncertain coordination with his pick-up bands, rendered Sly's comeback less certain than others in the same year by the formerly acrimonious reggae-rockers the Police, the revamped Van Halen, and the once-wild Led Zeppelin. Agent Steve Green, fielding some offers on Sly's behalf, assured uncertain bookers and a Reuters reporter, "He can do it, but he's got to want to do it."

Looking back now on 2007, Sly believes his audiences "can tell that I'm not satisfied, by the way I walk off the stage. I do what I have to do, but I'm not satisfied, 'cause I'm not dealing with the people I will be dealing with in the near future. . . . Because it's money, we need more money to prepare. Then I'll get the people who are supposed to be there."

In song, Sly promised he'd be gone for a while, and he was. There are a lot of people who want him back, if only he wants it. "Now is the time to let your light shine," David Kapralik advises his former client, and he then applies some other memorable lyrics: "You can make it if you try. Are you ready?"

Afterword

I N FEBRUARY 2008, A LITTLE OVER a year after my first interview with Sly and several months after submitting the first draft of this book, I found myself summoned back to the wine country mansion that had become Sly's haven, workplace, and crash pad for such occasional old friends and partners in crime as George Clinton. Once again, the stalwart Neal Austinson rode shotgun with me through the hills of Northern California and provided an opportunity to reflect not only on what was happening with his friend Sly but also on the short- and long-term impact of the Family Stone's legacy.

We talked about how the Family Stone had been funky enough for Harlem and Watts, and trippy enough for the Haight-Ashbury. The band had also demonstrated that rock outfits could ride a hip groove, and that grooving dance bands could have the autonomous individuality of a rock outfit. The Family Stone could as easily generate good vibes in dance clubs and bedrooms as enthrall thousands at live concerts.

Part of Sly's power as songwriter had flowed through his lyrics, conveying politically and culturally cogent messages without being polemical, and thus clearing the way for forthright free-speechers, all the way up to Public Enemy and Tupac Shakur. Then there were the melodies and arrangements, in which Sly could position as many as five singing voices over a foundation of drum and bass, elaborated by guitar and horns and decorated with shouts, scats, and occasional electronic effects. This had served up a delicious alternative to power trios and hard-rocking quartets. And in resurrected form today on reissued recordings and by spin-off bands, it continued to put the shame to music manipulated through sound samples, synthesizers, and advanced computer programs.

When Neal and I arrived at Sly's place, we found he was already being visited by another long-time acquaintance, Charles Richardson. Charles had shot and produced documentaries for the History Channel and elsewhere and was very savvy about computers and their creative potential for music making, as well as about record production. He'd helped Sly and the recently visiting George Clinton lay down some tracks, and was hoping to help materialize Sly's own first album in twenty-six years, along with more live gigs. Observing Charles's artful manipulation of a laptop was Rikki Gordon, the San Francisco–based singer who'd partnered with Sly onstage the previous November in New York.

After the expected wait, Sly descended from an upper floor, comfortably dressed in loose clothing and a knit cap. He seemed in a mood befitting the warm, bright weather outside. In fact, he insisted on our leaving the mansion and getting the interview started inside his 1958 Packard, with him driving, so that he could take the classic car into town and get it washed. We walked out to the vehicle, which was stationed alongside the terraced vineyard. The Packard was colorful, shiny, and solid, the way rock 'n' roll was a long time ago.

This time around, Sly was comfortable having me record him. He was quite cogent and cordial, and he drove carefully along the narrow roads winding through the pastoral landscape.

He began by talking about social and political issues, noting that he'd never voted. "I've wanted to," he maintained, "but I never know who's who till after it's over. And everybody always switches up on me. I don't want to think that I voted for someone who's doin' shit." Regarding the 2008 Democratic primary, Sly offered, "I'm thinking that these Clintons would not be so likely to goof up too much. How could Bill and Hillary both do two fuckups?"

"The ability of people to fuck up repeatedly, in the same way, is incredible," I responded from the passenger seat. "It goes on a lot. And you never know when somebody is reformed. . . ."

Pause. Sly seemed unswerved, and I switched gears.

"If you were to get out there with the whole band or most of it, would you be wanting to play all the same music you played back then, or would you be wanting them to do some of your new music?" I knew he'd been hard at work upstairs in the mansion, particularly in the wee hours.

"It would have to be the new music as well."

"In the touring you've been doing since you and I talked at the beginning of last year, it seems like audiences are yelling for you to do the old stuff. Do you ever get a little tired of it?"

"Well, yeah, they like the old stuff, but they don't know any better, so it's up to me to get the new stuff recorded, to give them reason to want to say, 'Hey, what about the new stuff?' Until then, I'm glad they like the old stuff."

"You didn't get an album out last year. Will you have one out this year?"

"It really depends on some business that's gotta be dealt with first. It'll be on my label, or on Clive's [Davis], wherever Clive is. He hasn't committed himself; I just hope so. Clive is my favorite guy in the business. . . . It'll all come together, and there will be a lot of help, as soon as I get the records starting to be heard. That always attracts the concern of people that know how to do things for ya."

"What are you gonna have to ask for that you don't have already?"

He hesitated. "I don't know. Nowadays I don't know how they do it, as much as I used to. I'm gonna release some things on the Internet anyway, see what happens. David Bowie and everybody else, they do that. Gotta see what's up."

After a fuel stop, Sly turned the wheel over to Neal and repositioned himself on the backseat. I gave him a sealed envelope bearing his name, which had been presented to me in Hawaii by his former manager, David Kapralik. Sly chuckled, opened the envelope, and read the note.

"Ilili," he murmured. He'd noticed David's Hawaiian nickname, which translates literally as 'a blooming nut,' and is David's metaphor for a man who went to seed and has started to grow, and blossom, all over again. "That's the way it is," Sly added softly.

"I think he still sees you as soul mates."

"I like David."

"Any words you'd like me to pass back to him?"

"Tell him I said, 'Book a gig!'" Sly replied, smiling broadly.

"But could we get him off Maui?" I inquired rhetorically.

"Do the gig in Maui!"

I brought up my recent conversations with Sly's two female collaborators in his high school group, the Viscaynes. Charlene Imhoff Davidson, now a successful banker in nearby Napa, had told me, "I'd love to just sit down and talk with him . . . because I knew him when, that young man who was very caring and lovely and talented." Maria Boldway Douglas, living with her husband and granddaughter in Arizona, envisioned a get-together where "we'd probably just hug each other, and he'd give me that crazy, wicked smile, and we'd just start laughing."

"I'm finding person after person who has lots of love for you," I tell Sly, "like Charlene and Maria—"

"Ria Boldway!" Sly exclaimed, recalling her maiden name. "Where's she now?"

"She's in Arizona, married for the second time, still singing."

"Yeah!" Sly sighed warmly. "They're good people. I gotta get their numbers from you."

"What would you want to give to those folks?"

"Just new stuff. That's all I have."

The old but proud Packard pulled into the car wash of Sly's choice.

"Did it feel like a big change, moving up here from L.A.?"

"Yeah, but I welcomed the change. I get to make my own schedule, pretty much."

"Why couldn't you do that in L.A.?" Of course, I'd heard and read plenty of reports about the various levels of distraction in those years down there.

" 'Cause everybody had something to do with what time I was supposed to be wherever," Sly responded, with an elusive chuckle. "Up here it's pretty fair, pretty even."

"And you don't get too lonely?"

"I can stimulate excitement," Sly assured, "or I can just kick back and watch other things go."

"And when you're kicking back," I persisted, "what are you paying attention to, what turns you on?"

He gazed out the window at some of the car wash customers hanging around the facility. "Like those girls waiting over there," Sly chortled. "Wait, I'm gonna go inside, I'll be back."

He ambled off in the general direction of the local ladies. I'd been alerted to Sly's tendency to disappear and reappear on whim, so I wasn't surprised when he didn't return. Using his cell phone, he'd secured a separate ride home from Rikki Gordon, leaving Neal and me to pilot the Packard back to the mansion. After another wait there, I got to continue the chat across the kitchen table, with Rikki witnessing. Sly's departed parents, K. C. and Alpha Stewart, also looked on, smiling from a color photograph placed under a luxuriant vase of flowers nearby.

"If you go back to stuff like 'Life,' it sounds like you were writing about yourself. Is that true nowadays? Is it about what you're learning and feeling?"

"Or what I'm imagining. It's all the time about myself. Basically, I don't care what nobody says or nothin'. If I didn't get the most out of something, I wouldn't do it."

What I've seen of Sly performing live and on YouTube over the past year hasn't convinced me that he's been getting the most out of his music. "It seems to me that I haven't been hearing enough of you playing your keyboard," I tell him.

"They couldn't afford to take roadies and get the right equipment, and do a lot of the things required for me to be ready to play. I don't mind workin' but I ain't gonna work like that again."

"So you'll be doing more singing and playing during your sets?"

"Yeah, I will, I will, it's just a matter of money, and at the same time letting everybody know that I don't mind showing up on time *every* night, if necessary. You know what I mean?"

"Your health is good?"

"I feel good, I feel much better."

"If you had to choose, what do you think is your best album?"

Sly chuckled. "The next one. And that's what I really think."

"What kind of songs are we gonna hear on it?"

"The latest one goes, let's see . . . *I'm the real model / And I ain't the role model / I got a dog named Duck with a stroll-waddle / If I see you in the desert, I got the cold bottle / 'cause I'm the real model / I ain't the role model.*" He smiled, hoping his self-appreciation was being shared. "I like to not have people try to make me a role model. I don't like that, 'cause I don't think anybody should have that burden. Everybody's gotta be a role model, either everybody or nobody. You know what I mean?"

"So that's been a burden on you?"

"Yeah. If something happens that they don't choose to appreciate, then comes the role model thing. 'You're a role model, what happens when *you* get in trouble?' O. J. Simpson did." He snickered. "And I didn't do *near* that kind of stuff. Aargh! Can't even describe that."

After some jocular exchanges with Rikki, Charles, Neal and me, Sly announced, "I'm gonna go now, okay?" and headed back up the stairs, shouting, "Thank you!"

Selected Discography

P RESENTED HERE IS AN OVER-
view of the major Sly & the Family
Stone LP reissues on CD, as well as
reissues and compilations currently available featuring Sly with
and without the original and later formations of the Family Stone.
The first seven Sly & the Family Stone albums all include bonus
tracks in their remastered, reissued formats. Some of those tracks
are monophonic singles versions of album tracks, and others are
previously unreleased. Each track is included in the commentary
for each album, all of which are gathered in *The Collection* box
(2007). Aside from the albums included here, there are recordings
of festival performances at Woodstock, Isle of Wight, and Atlanta,
and several excellent bootlegs recorded at the Fillmore East in 1968
and at the Kasteel Groeneveld in Baarn, the Netherlands, in 1970.
The Fillmore recordings may finally be remastered and released by
Sony in 2009. Worth viewing are two DVD's, *My Own Beliefs:
Video Anthology 1969–1986* (two discs) and *It's a Family Affair*
(single disc). Both are collections of performances, televised
appearances, and promotional videos, mostly from the band's

heyday and showcasing the hits, but also with some scenes of Sly interacting with TV hosts and guests. The recording quality is less than ideal, but the depiction of the evolution and presentation of the group and its leader is fascinating. There are numerous bootlegs of Sly's pre–Family Stone material and early band demos, and of later assemblages, generally of inferior quality and put out on a variety of pirate labels available from various sources, many of which can be found on the Internet. With all such bootlegs, *caveat emptor.*

Not covered here are Starbucks's Hear Music *Higher* compilation, a decent point-of-sale primer for the uninitiated, and *Different Strokes*, a 2005 collection of Sly classics reworked, not always to good effect, by "different folks."

SLY & THE FAMILY STONE

A Whole New Thing Epic, 1967

> (1) Underdog; (2) If This Room Could Talk; (3) Run, Run, Run; (4) Turn Me Loose; (5) Let Me Hear It from You; (6) Advice; (7) I Cannot Make It; (8) Trip to Your Heart; (9) I Hate to Love Her; (10) Bad Risk; (11) That Kind of Person; (12) Dog; *Bonus Tracks:* (13) Underdog (single version); (14) Let Me Hear It from You (single version); (15) Only One Way Out of This Mess; (16) What Would I Do; (17) You Better Help Yourself (instrumental)

> Sly Stone—vocals, keyboards, guitar, bass; Rose Stone— keyboards, vocals; Freddie Stone—guitar, vocals; Cynthia Robinson—trumpet; Larry Graham—bass, vocals; Jerry Martini—saxophone, vocals; Greg Errico—drums

There was a lot on this disc, perhaps too much for any radio programmer, record store owner, or listener to be able to divine what the "thing" was, other than that it was being performed by a talented collection of players and singers, led by an already experienced songwriter and arranger. Like many Family Stone sides, it started strong, with a message song ("Underdog") that could be counted as one of Sly's few references to racial discrimination. Musically there were references back to the R & B approach of Autumn Records (and to the spirit of Otis Redding), and ahead to funk, psychedelia, and the dynamics and colors of the hit singles. Larry got a solo soul-vocal outing on "Let Me Hear It from You," one of several aspects of this debut disc that wouldn't be repeated in the band's later work. The bonus tracks showcased wild horn harmonies on "Only One Way Out of This Mess" and the ahead-of-its-time instrumental fusion of "You Better Help Yourself."

Dance to the Music Epic, 1968

(1) Dance to the Music; (2) Higher; (3) I Ain't Got Nobody (For Real); (4) Dance to the Medley: (a) Music Is Alive, (b) Dance In, (c) Music Lover; (5) Ride the Rhythm; (6) Color Me True; (7) Are You Ready; (8) Don't Burn Baby; (9) I'll Never Fall in Love Again; *Bonus Tracks:* (10) Dance to the Music (single version); (11) Higher (unissued single version); (12) Soul Clappin'; (13) We Love All; (14) I Can't Turn You Loose; (15) Never Do Your Woman Wrong

Sly Stone—vocals, keyboards, guitar; Rose Stone—keyboards, vocals; Freddie Stone—guitar, vocals; Cynthia Robinson—trumpet; Larry Graham—bass, vocals; Jerry Martini—saxophone, vocals; Greg Errico—drums

The imperative of the title track proved both attractive and easy for fans to follow up on, an invitation to come celebrate and party with this bi-racial, bi-gender band that was new on the scene. The extended "Medley," like "Dance," served to introduce the individual members of the Family Stone and also to affirm their collective fun and ensemble strength, with flashes of psychedelia and phase shifting. Not all the tracks are equally memorable, but the single and the album earned the band a place on rock radio and in stores. The previously unreleased "We Love All" contains the kind of social messaging apparent on several later hits. "I Can't Turn You Loose" exhibits a tight horn-rhythm connection evocative of Otis Redding. "Soul Clappin'" suggests what the B-52's would mine for retro fun three decades later.

Life Epic, 1968

(1) Dynamite!; (2) Chicken; (3) Plastic Jim; (4) Fun; (5) Into My Own Thing; (6) Harmony; (7) Life; (8) Love City; (9) I'm an Animal; (10) M'Lady; (11) Jane Is a Groupee; *Bonus Tracks:* (12) Dynamite! (single version); (13) Seven More Days; (14) Pressure; (15) Sorrow

Sly Stone—vocals, keyboards, guitar; Rose Stone—keyboards, vocals; Freddie Stone—guitar, vocals; Cynthia Robinson—trumpet; Larry Graham—bass, vocals; Jerry Martini—saxophone; Greg Errico—drums

Listened to now, it's hard to tell why *Life* was so overshadowed by its predecessor, because in many ways it's a brighter record. "Fun," "Life," and "Love City" were as catchy as "Dance to the Music," with even more of Sly's "message" lyrics. "M'Lady" was a catchy valentine. And there was much humor and delight in "Chicken," "I'm an Animal," and "Jane Is a Groupee." The group continued to showcase its broad, confident embrace of R & B, funk, psychedelia, and pop dance music.

Stand! Epic, 1969

(1) Stand!; (2) Don't Call Me Nigger, Whitey; (3) I Want to Take You Higher; (4) Somebody's Watching You; (5) Sing a Simple Song; (6) Everyday People; (7) Sex Machine; (8) You Can Make It If You Try; *Bonus Tracks:* (9) Stand! (single version); (10) I Want to Take You Higher (single version); (11) You Can Make It If You Try (unissued single version); (12) Soul Clappin'; (13) My Brain (Zig-Zag)

Sly Stone—vocals, keyboards, guitar; Rose Stone—keyboards, vocals; Freddie Stone—guitar, vocals; Cynthia Robinson—trumpet; Larry Graham—bass, vocals; Jerry Martini—saxophone, vocals; Greg Errico—drums

The grooves laid down on earlier discs became stronger and more sophisticated on *Stand!*, and Sly's mastery of pop poetry proved unmatchable and irresistible, resulting in four hit songs within one dynamic album. Aside from the hits, there was the forthright, somber sound of "Don't Call Me Nigger, Whitey," a precursor of *Riot*, and the blue psychedelia of "Sex Machine." With more message than perhaps any other rock record outside the folk/rock genre, *Stand!* was also a paradigm of arrangement and production.

Greatest Hits Epic, 1970

(1) I Want to Take You Higher; (2) Everybody Is a Star; (3) Stand!; (4) Life; (5) Fun; (6) You Can Make It If You Try; (7) Dance to the Music; (8) Everyday People; (9) Hot Fun in the Summertime; (10) M'Lady; (11) Sing a Simple Song; (12) Thank You (Falettinme Be Mice Elf Agin)

Sly Stone—vocals, keyboards, guitar; Rose Stone—keyboards, vocals; Freddie Stone—guitar, vocals; Cynthia Robinson—trumpet; Larry Graham—bass, vocals; Jerry Martini—saxophone, vocals; Greg Errico—drums

This compilation served well to get a lot of the band's best music to date out to a lot of people, and also to fill the elongated gap between new albums. Included were two songs, very different from each other, that didn't appear on any other album: "Hot Fun in the Summertime" and "Thank You." The first was an atypically jazzy laid-back groove, the second a funky jump with shady lyrics, both ahead of their time and ultimately influential on music to come

from other artists. The rest of the album constitutes a showcase of
the Family Stone's most upbeat material.

There's a Riot Goin' On Epic, 1971
> (1) Luv N' Haight; (2) Just Like a Baby; (3) Poet; (4) Family
> Affair; (5) Africa Talks to You "The Asphalt Jungle"; (6) There's a
> Riot Goin' On; (7) Brave & Strong; (8) (You Caught Me) Smilin';
> (9) Time; (10) Spaced Cowboy; (11) Runnin' Away; (12) Thank
> You for Talkin' to Me Africa; *Bonus Tracks:* (13) Runnin' Away
> (single version); (14) My Gorilla Is My Butler; (15) Do You Know
> What?; (16) That's Pretty Clean
>
> Sly Stone—vocals, keyboards, guitar; Rose Stone—keyboards,
> vocals; Freddie Stone—guitar, vocals; Cynthia Robinson—
> trumpet; Larry Graham—bass, vocals; Jerry Martini—
> saxophone, vocals; Greg Errico—drums; Bobby
> Womack—guitar; Billy Preston—keyboards; Miles Davis, Herbie
> Hancock, Ike Turner, Jim Ford, Joe Hicks—miscellaneous
> contributions

The dissolution of the original flesh-and-blood Family Stone and
Sly's shift of focus toward himself and toward the drum machine
were readily apparent on this iconic album, as was a generally
darker and funkier approach to the music suggestive of the impact
of harder drugs and personal strife. The rhythms, human and electronic, were often artful and suggestive of what would later be
heard from Sly and other musicians, notably Stevie Wonder and
Prince, but the melody lines were much narrower and the song list
less diverse than on the Family Stone's earlier albums. There are
moments of lyrical strength and humor, notable on "Family
Affair," *Riot*'s chart-topping single, and on "Spaced Cowboy."
Among the bonus tracks are three instrumentals, which show
more about how Sly was working deep in grooves and forming up
his funk.

Fresh Epic, 1973

(1) In Time; (2) If You Want Me to Stay; (3) Let Me Have It All; (4) Frisky; (5) Thankful N' Thoughtful; (6) Skin I'm In; (7) I Don't Know (Satisfaction); (8) Keep On Dancin'; (9) Que Sera, Sera (Whatever Will Be, Will Be); (10) If It Were Left Up to Me; (11) Babies Makin' Babies; *Bonus Tracks:* (12) Let Me Have It All (alternate mix); (13) Frisky (alternate mix); (14) Skin I'm In (alternate mix); (15) Keep On Dancin' (alternate mix); (16) Babies Makin' Babies (alternate version)

Sly Stone—vocals, keyboards, guitar, bass; Rose Stone—keyboards, vocals; Freddie Stone—guitar; Cynthia Robinson—trumpet; Rustee Allen—bass; Larry Graham—bass; Jerry Martini—saxophone; Pat Rizzo—saxophone; Andy Newmark—drums; Vet Stone, Mary McCreary, Elva Mouton—backing vocals

Without ever achieving the antiheroic landmark status of *Riot*, this album was arguably more user-friendly, engaging, and wider reaching than its predecessor, while continuing to probe the potential of funk and electronically manipulated rhythms and editing. Tracks like "In Time" were sophisticated, "Let Me Have It All" made soulful use of its Little Sister female chorus, and "If You Want Me to Stay" was as alluring and personal as anything Sly had ever laid down. The surprising (and spuriously controversial) cover of "Que Sera, Sera" evoked Sly and Rose's sacred roots. Overall, this seemed a brief reprise of good sounds, if not good times. The bonus tracks are reflective of Sly's increasing involvement in studio retakes, striving toward some private standard of satisfaction; they're all good, but what ended up on the album is better.

Small Talk Epic, 1974

(1) Small Talk; (2) Say You Will; (3) Mother Beautiful; (4) Time for Livin'; (5) Can't Strain My Brain; (6) Loose Booty; (7) Holdin' On; (8) Wishful Thinkin'; (9) Better Thee Than Me; (10) Livin' While I'm Livin'; (11) This Is Love; *Bonus Tracks:* (12) Crossword

Puzzle (early version); (13) Time for Livin' (alternate version); (14) Loose Booty (alternate version); (15) Positive

Sly Stone—vocals, keyboards, guitar, bass; Rose Stone Banks—keyboards, vocals; Freddie Stone—guitar, vocals; Cynthia Robinson—trumpet; Rustee Allen—bass; Bill Lordan—drums; Vet Stone—vocals, keyboards; Jerry Martini—saxophone; Pat Rizzo—flute, saxophone; Sid Page—violin; Kathy Silva, Sly Stone Jr.—background vocals

Technically this was the last Sly & the Family Stone album, but there was little left of the original group's sound, most of whose members had either departed or had been placed in subsidiary roles. Although some of the newer players were musically talented, the material Sly gave them for this project had little of his familiar songwriting sparkle, and the layering in of strings did little to dress up the lackluster arrangements and the quirky production. Rustee Allen helped perk up the livelier tracks, "Loose Booty" and "Livin' While I'm Livin'," and "Mother Beautiful" suggested an upbeat approach to family life, in a mode that Stevie Wonder would later borrow. The alternate version of "Time for Livin'" sounded rather ragged with the syrupy strings fading in and out, but on "Positive," you can hear drummer Bill Lordan making good use of what he said Sly taught him about funk.

SLY STONE

High on You Epic, 1975

(1) I Get High on You; (2) Crossword Puzzle; (3) That's Lovin' You; (4) Who Do You Love?; (5) Green Eyed Monster Girl; (6) Organize; (7) Le Lo Li; (8) My World; (9) So Good to Me; (10). Greed

Sly Stone—vocals, keyboards, guitar, bass; Freddie Stone—guitar, vocals; Cynthia Robinson—trumpet, vocals; Jerry Martini—saxophone; Dennis Marcellino—saxophone; Rustee Allen—bass;

Bobby Vega—bass; Gail Muldrow—guitar; Bill Lordan, Michael Samuels, Jim Strassburg, Willie Sparks—drums; Bobby Lyles, Truman Thomas—keyboards; Dawn Silva, Elva Mouton, Vet Stewart, Rudy Love—background vocals

Epic dropped the Family Stone name from this album, though some of the band's members continued to contribute, alongside a host of others. The material itself harkened back to the message mission of the Family Stone classics, on tracks such as "Organize," "Le Lo Li," and "Greed." Sly's vocals retrieved some of their liveliness and mischief, and at times he's every bit as good as any contemporary offering by Smokey Robinson or Marvin Gaye. (Smokey's chart-topping "Cruisin'," from 1979, sounded a lot like this album's "My World," from four years earlier, though Sly's song was prettier.) The high spirits and artful arrangements on this album deserved the kind of recognition that Sly may not have been in condition to follow up on, aside from the fact that his declining public image overshadowed the album's quality and uniqueness.

Heard Ya Missed Me, Well I'm Back Epic, 1976
(1) Heard Ya Missed Me, Well I'm Back; (2) What Was I Thinkin' in My Head; (3) Nothing Less Than Happiness; (4) Sexy Situation; (5) Blessing in Disguise; (6) Everything in You; (7) Mother Is a Hippie; (8) Let's Be Together; (9) The Thing; (10) Family Again

Sly Stone—vocals, keyboards; Cynthia Robinson—trumpet; Dwight Hogan—bass, vocals; Anthony Warren—drums; Joseph Baker—guitar, vocals; John Colla—saxophone; Steve Schuster—saxophone, flute; John Farey—keyboards, trombone; Armando Peraza—percussion; Lady Bianca—lead and background vocals, clavinet; Dawn Weber, Virginia Ayers—percussion, background vocals; Vicki Blackwell—violin; Peter Frampton—guitar

In its overall sound and happy tone and in the look of the back-cover photograph, this project was evocative of a '60s or '70s musical along the lines of *Hair* or *Jesus Christ Superstar*. From the opening title track on, there was much involvement of the chorus and relatively little of Sly's solo voice. An exception was "Nothing Less Than Happiness," which showcased, more than just about any other song in his canon, Sly's mastery of vocal phrasing and texture; it was a homage to doo-wop and early rock that was fabulously well written, arranged, and performed. Among the musicians drawn to the making of this album were veteran conguero Armando Peraza and rock guitarist Peter Frampton, riding the crest of the hits he'd scored that year. As with *High on* You, the disc did not have as strong a draw on record buyers, but both albums are worth the price of the imported CDs, which is pretty much the only way you'll get them now.

Back on the Right Track Warner Brothers, 1979

(1) Remember Who You Are; (2) Back on the Right Track; (3). If It's Not Addin' Up; (4) The Same Thing (Makes You Laugh, Makes You Cry); (5) Shine It On; (6) It Takes All Kinds; (7) Who's to Say?; (8) Sheer Energy

Sly Stone—vocals, keyboards, harmonica; Freddie Stone—guitar, vocals; Joseph Baker—guitar; Hamp Banks—guitar; Cynthia Robinson—trumpet; Keni Burke—bass; Alvin Taylor—drums; Walter Downing—keyboards; Mark Davis—keyboards; Ollie Brown—percussion; Pat Rizzo—saxophone; Steve Madaio, Fred Smith, Gary Herbig—horns; Rose Stone Banks, Lisa Banks—backing vocals

Sly seemed to have left much of his tunefulness behind, at least for the time being, when he departed the Epic label and made this first of two albums for Warner. In his lyrics, he retained some of his cleverness and his telegraphed insightful messages, most creatively applied in fine funky fashion on "The Same Thing" and "It Takes All Kinds." The sound was evocative of James Brown and predictive of Prince, and at its worst was still better than much of the rock and R & B from this and the following decade. Sly's one-time mentor and long-time associate Hamp "Bubba" Banks was credited as associate producer and guitarist, and Rose, Sly's sister and Bubba's wife at the time, provided backing vocals alongside her daughter, Lisa.

Ain't but the One Way Warner Brothers, 1982

(1) L.O.V.I.N.U.; (2) One Way; (3) Ha Ha, Hee Hee; (4) Hobo Ken; (5) Who in the Funk Do You Think You Are; (6) You Really Got Me; (7) Sylvester; (8) We Can Do It; (9) High, Y'All

Sly Stone—vocals, keyboards; Pat Rizzo—saxophone; George Clinton—miscellaneous contributions

This proved a somewhat better showcase of Sly's eclectic talent than did the earlier Warner effort, but the overproduction rather quashed the superior quality of the songs. The lush arrangements evinced what was being borrowed from Sly by groups like Earth, Wind & Fire, and "Who in the Funk Do You Think You Are" sounded almost suited to the catchy, repetitive mode of disco, which had "died" a couple years earlier. The album could have used more of the sort of fun and funk abounding in Sly's imaginative cover of the Kinks' "You Really Got Me." The two Warner releases were the last to bear the Family Stone moniker (so far), though the band had no apparent connection with the final album other than the involvement of its former leader.

COMPILATIONS

Precious Stone: In the Studio with Sly Stone 1963–1965 Ace, 1994

What's precious here are some of the raw elements and skills that Sly assembled while working as an in-house songwriter, arranger, and producer for San Francisco's Autumn Records in the early

1960s. Assembled and meticulously annotated by Alec Palao, the singles, not all of which made it onto finished LPs, feature the singing and/or playing of Sly, siblings Freddie and Rose, George & Teddy (Jerry Martini's sometime employers), Billy Preston, and Autumn star Bobby Freeman. Sly deals easily in R & B, early soul, and pop modes, at one point laying down a bit of jazz scat. Just as Led Zeppelin's Jimmy Page drew on his former life as a session guitarist, Sly's audible technical and musical discipline would go gold with the Family Stone.

The Essential Sly & the Family Stone Sony, 2002

For those not wanting to buy or to carry around the big *Collection* box, this is an excellent remastered two-disc, thirty-five-track alternative, including not only all the hits (with notation of their placement on the charts) but also some of the best of the other Epic tracks, dating back to *A Whole New Thing* and ahead to *High on You*. It's arguably the best way for a listener to grasp the scope of Sly and the band's history.

Sly & the Family Stone: The Collection Sony, 2007

The first seven LPs released by Epic under the Sly & the Family Stone moniker were collected in this box by Sony in 2007. All albums include bonus tracks and new liner notes by various contemporary rock commentators alongside the pleasingly remastered original tracks and notes. The bonus tracks feature singles versions of the hit songs, some of them in mono, and some good and revealing music not previously available to the public (accounted for in the discussion of the individual albums, above).

Sources

ALTHOUGH THE FOLLOWING includes numerous magazine and newspaper articles written about the Family Stone and/or Sly in a broad or specific context, there have been only two previous books dealing with the band with any biographical significance. Joel Selvin's *Oral History*, part of a series of similar books edited by Dave Marsh, is a collection of quotes from all band members except Sly and from related parties, and Miles Marshall Lewis's *There's a Riot Goin' On* focuses on the album of its title, with brief biographical material about Sly.

BOOKS

Amende, Coral. *Rock Confidential.* New York: Plume, 2000.

Bacon, Tony. *The Bass Book: An Illustrated History of the Bass Guitar.* San Francisco: Miller Freeman, 1995.

Braun, Eric. *Doris Day.* London: Weidenfeld and Nicolson, 1991.

Clifford, Mike, ed. *The Illustrated Encyclopedia of Black Music.* New York: Harmony, 1982.

Davis, Miles, with Quincy Troupe. *Miles: The Autobiography.* New York: Simon and Schuster, 1989.

Denyer, Ralph. *The Guitar Handbook.* New York: Alfred A. Knopf, 1996.

Herman, Gary. *Rock 'n' roll Babylon.* London: Plexus, 1994.

Jonnes, Jill. *Hep-Cats, Narcs, and Pipe Dreams: A History of America's Romance with Illegal Drugs.* New York: Scribner, 1996.

Larkin, Colin. *The Virgin Encyclopedia of Dance Music.* London: Virgin, 1998.

Lewis, Miles Marshall. *Sly and the Family Stone's* There's a Riot Goin' On. New York: Continuum, 2006.

Marcus, Greil. *Mystery Train: Images of America in Rock 'n' roll Music.* New York: E. P. Dutton, 1975.

Marsh, Dave, and Kevin Stein. *The Book of Rock Lists.* New York: Dell, 1984.

Miller, Jim, ed. *The Rolling Stone Illustrated History of Rock & Roll.* New York: Random House, 1976.

Santana, Deborah. *Space Between the Stars: My Journey to an Open Heart.* New York: One World/Ballantine, 2006.

Selvin, Joel. *Sly and the Family Stone: An Oral History.* New York: Harper, 1998.

Verna, Paul, ed. *The Encyclopedia of Record Producers.* New York: Billboard, 1999.

Vincent, Rickey. *Funk: The Music, the People, and the Rhythm of the One.* New York: St. Martin's Griffin, 1996.

Whitburn, Joel. *The Billboard Book of Top 40 Albums.* New York: Billboard, 1987.

Wills, Maury, and Mike Celizic: *On the Run: The Never Dull and Often Shocking Life of Maury Wills.* New York: Carroll and Graf, 1991.

FILMS

Dance to the Music. Willen Alkema and Edwin and Arno Konings, 2008.
The Skin I'm In (rough cut). Daedalus Productions, 2000.

MAGAZINE ARTICLES

Aletti, Vince. "There's a Riot Goin' On (review)." *Rolling Stone*, December 23, 1971.

Blashill, Pat, et al. "Fresh: Sly and the Family Stone." *Rolling Stone*, December 11, 2003: 138.

Bozza, Anthony. "Sly and the New Family Member." *Rolling Stone*, August 6, 1998: 31.

Edwards, Gavin. "The Essential Sly and the Family Stone." *Rolling Stone*, April 17, 2003: 109.

Fong-Torres, Ben. "Everybody Is a Star: Travels with Sly Stone." *Rolling Stone,* March 19, 1970.

Gore, Joe. "Old School Cool: A '70s Funk Lesson." *Guitar Player*, September 1994: 47–54.

Graff, Gary. "Sly and the Family Stone: Stand!" *Guitar World*, June 1999: 61.

Hiestand, Jesse. "Backstage at the Grammys." *The Hollywood Reporter*, February 9, 2006: 37.

Jisi, Chris. "Sly & the Family Stone's 'If You Want Me to Stay'—Rustee Allen's Complete Bass Line." *Bass Player*, October 2006: 78.

Kamp, David. "Sly Stone's Higher Power." *Vanity Fair*, August 2007: 136–184.

Keegan, Rebecca Winters. "Reclusive Star Emerges, Has New Haircut." *Time*, February 20, 2006: 71.

Leslie, Jimmy. "Larry Graham: Trunk of the Funk Tree." *Bass Player*, May 2007: 30–37.

Marcus, Greil. "There's a Riot Goin' On: Muzak with Its Finger on the Trigger." *Creem*, April 1972: 14.

Novak, Ralph, and Todd Gold. "The Decline and Fall of Sly Stone." *People*, June 17, 1996: 139–143.

Orth, Maureen. "A Family Affair—for 23,000." *Newsweek*, June 17, 1974: 62

Selvin, Joel. "Lucifer Rising." *Mojo*, August 2001: 80–91.

"Sly's Arena Wedding." *Rolling Stone*, May 19, 2005: 26.

"Sly Stone's Heart of Darkness." *Spin*, December 1985: 44–67.

Trow, George W. S. "The Biggest Event This Year." *The New Yorker*, August 26, 1974: 30–45.

Was, Don. "Sly and the Family Stone." *Rolling Stone*, April 15, 2004: 132.

Wilkinson, Peter. "Sly's Strange Comeback." *Rolling Stone*, March 9, 2006: 17–20.

NEWSPAPER ARTICLES

"Arrest Warrant Issued for Rock Singer Sly Stone." *The Vancouver Sun*, December 10, 1987: F-4.

Bracelin, Jason. "Sly Comes in from the Cold." *Las Vegas Review-Journal*, April 2, 2007.

Carey, Derek. "Sly Stone Takes Stand for Comebacks." *Reuters News Agency*, November 22, 2007.

Concert review. *De Standaard* (Gossetlaan, Belgium), July 16, 2007.

Concert review. *Free!* (magazine), July 21, 2007.

Concert review. *TV5 Monde* (Nice, France), July 20, 2007.

"Daley Says Rioting at Rock Concert Was Planned." *New York Times*, July 29, 1970.

Du Lac, J. Freedom. "Sly Stone's Surprise." *Washington Post*, January 27, 2006.

Kaliss, Jeff. "Stone Is at Work but He Keeps It on the Sly." *Los Angeles Times*, January 9, 2007.

Katsilometes, John. "How George Wallace Aligned the Stars to Coerce One Big Star to Perform at Flamingo Las Vegas." *Las Vegas Sun*, April 2, 2007.

Lacey, Liam. "Sly's Abortive Concert a Sad Embarrassment." *Toronto Globe and Mail*, March 6, 1982: E-3.

O'Hagan, Sean. "I Want to Take You . . . Lower." *The Observer* (London, England), July 15, 2007.

Pond, Steve. Concert review. *Los Angeles Times*, November 13, 1987.

Quillen, Shay. "Sly Stone Shows Up, Goes Nowhere Fast in San Jose Concert." *San Jose Mercury-News*, July 8, 2007.

Saneh, Kelefa. "For $103.35, You Take What You Can Get." *New York Times*, November 22, 2007.

Schmitter, Blaise. "Sly's First European Club Performance: Overwhelming!" *Funk-U* (magazine) (Paris, France), July 24, 2007.

Selvin, Joel. "Sly Stone Takes the Stage, but the Flair Is a No-Show." *San Francisco Chronicle*, July 9, 2007.

Senff, Boris. Concert review. *Le Temps* (Geneva, Switzerland), July 15, 2007.

"Sly and the Family Stone Plays to a Sell-Out Crowd at Garden." *New York Times*, September 12, 1971: 94.

"Sly Opens Series at Radio City to an Unimpressed Audience." *New York Times*, January 18, 1975.

"Sly Stone Jailed on Drug Charges." *The Ottawa Citizen*, February 19, 1987: E-2.

"Sly Stone Jailed for Illegal Gun." *Toronto Globe and Mail*, February 10, 1983: 23.

"Stone Jailed on Theft Charge." *Toronto Globe and Mail*, August 20, 1983: E-2.

"3 Shot in Chicago During Rock Riot." *New York Times*, July 28, 1970: 1.

Wallace, George. "Sly Joins the Family Stone for His First Show in Two Decades, As Wallace's Special Guest." *PR Newswire*, April 2, 2007.

WEB SITES

www.airchexx.com (Sly deejaying on KSOL, 1967)

www.cogic.org (Church of God in Christ)

www.dentoncounty.com (Denton County, Texas)

www.drummerworld.com (Drummerworld)

www.familystonemusic.com (Jerry Martini and the Family Stone Project [band]) www.members.shaw.ca/stevesplace/BLinterview.htm (Bill Lordan interview)

www.myspace.com/gregerrico (Greg Errico)

www.phattadatta.com (promoted as "Sly Stone's personal site")

www.rosestoneuniverse.com (Rose Stone)

www.rusteeallen.com (Rustee Allen)

www.slyandthefamilystone.net (Will Odell, fan in England)

www.slyslilsis.com (Vet Stone)

www.slystonebook.com (Arno and Edwin Konings, *Thank You* [2009])

www.slystonemusic.com (Sony BMG Music Online)

www.stonecisum.com (Freddie Stone/Rev. Frederick Stewart)

www.woodstock69.com (1969 Woodstock Festival and Concert)

Acknowledgments

THE BEST THING ABOUT WRITing about music, apart from the music and the writing themselves, is meeting and talking with musicians, and with the people inside their lives and the business. There were challenges in assembling this book, but it was tugged along the long route to publication by the following people, for whom mention here is my way of saying thank you.

Some of you not only went on the record, but also provided info and recommendations that connected me with others. Gratitude for that goes to Jerry Martini, the earliest of my Family Stone contacts, and to Neal Austinson, who helped prompt my interview with Sly, his first in ages, and our second talk more than a year later. The Neal Austinson Archives were the source of much valuable material and information, and Neal helped put me in touch with a couple of other admirable archivists, known fondly as "The Dutch Twins" by many in these pages. Those indefatigable brothers, Edwin and Arno Konings, provided much in the way of general and specific info while continuing work on their own magnum opus, *Thank You*, due out within the next year or so.

Closer to home, San Franciscan Joel Selvin supplied transcriptions, recordings, and a revealing personal interview, alongside his own *Oral History*, heretofore the only interview-based book about Sly and the band.

It was Ric Stewart, with his fine eclectic web site there1.com, who first got me writing about Sly, and that's what attracted the attention of literary agent Robert Lecker, who connected me with the book's publisher. My dear friend Jann Moorhead provided informal legal counsel during the launch of the project and the occasionally rough waters later on. For background on the inspiring history of African Americans and Sylvester Stewart's roots in Denton, Texas, there were Denton denizens Lynette and Betty Kimble, Sly's cousin Christine McAdams, and the tireless Kim Cupit. Professor William Issel and his graduate student Richard John Figone moved the history forward and westward to mid-century Vallejo, California. Tender memories of that time and place were voiced by several dear souls, including venerated teacher Dave Froehlich and Ria Boldway Douglas, whose honesty and passion are a model for us all. My fortuitous flat tire at the side of a Marin County freeway led to a chance meeting with drummer James Henry, who later led me to singer Skyler Jett, who in turn led me to little sister Vet Stone. Appreciation for similar serendipity goes to hairstylist Eric Hooten, who led me to fellow stylist Bobby Gomez, who led me to Mario Errico.

The Errico family shared two generations of hospitality and garrulousness passed down from parents Jo and Nick to brothers Mario (another of my links to Sly) and Greg (the second of my cooperative veterans of the Family Stone). A similarly generous Italian American, Rich Romanello, told me of the Family Stone's early days and arranged for valuable accommodations in Southern California. The spirit of hospitality extended to the island of Maui, where Nancy and George Kahumoku Jr. put me up during my extended interviews with the magical David Kapralik (and sourced my side story on slack key guitar for *Guitar Player* magazine).

To those who wouldn't talk openly or at all for this book, some due to residual resentment over perceived past misrepresentations by writers and journalists, I can only express regret that you weren't able to appear more directly in this story. I hope that I'll have more to share with you some day. To all, including Sly, who shared their stories, I hope you feel properly accounted for.

The staff of the Art, Music, and Recreation Center of the San Francisco Public Library helped keep me informed, and Susan and the wizards at Castro Computer Services kept my cybermill turning. My collection of Sly & the Family Stone sides was bolstered by Streetlight Records, Amazon, John Hagelston of Rhino, and Tom Cording of Sony/Legacy. Invaluable detail and opinions about music, and the Family Stone in particular, came from rock and funk scholars Ben Fong-Torres, Alec Palao, and Rickey Vincent, as well as developmental editor George Case, and more informally from Bay Area music veteran Anthony Reginato of Mission Market. The book has been illuminated by multiple suppliers of photographs, both professional and amateur, among them the artful Jim Marshall and Steve Paley. Seth Affoumado and Beverly Tharp took useful portraits of the author. Alongside Neal Austinson, continued contact with Sly was facilitated by his other devoted helpmates, Charles Richardson and Rikki Gordon.

On the opposite coast, at mission control, aka Hal Leonard/ Backbeat Books, acquiring editor John Cerullo somehow managed to keep me in orbit, with reassuring words in my telephone earpiece and my e-mail inbox, and manuscript editor Mike Edison guided me in making my own written words look like a rock book, ready to be polished by copy editor Godwin Chu. Production editor Bernadette Malavarca completed the assembly, and Diane Levinson and Aaron Lefkove helped position the result in the public eye.

I bear a long and deep personal debt to my hometown and college papers, the *Bar Harbor Times* and the *Boston University News*, for first turning me on to journalism, and to the *Noe Valley Voice* for much later sparking a flashback that turned into a career, faithfully supported in more than one sense by my wife and conscience, Louise Whitlock. Our dancing and singing children, Natalie and Nicholas Kaliss, and our cat, Tula, have made the Kaliss Family Affair into a wonderful way to work hard while staying in touch with the other duties and delights of the world.

Index

"C'mon and Swim" (song), 22–24, 27, 140
Cole, Ruby, 3–4
Collection, The (box set), 170, 183, 194
Collins, Bootsy, 56, 131
Columbia Records, 44–46, 50, 52–53, 60, 74, 83, 91, 93, 97, 101, 104, 105, 115, 121
Commodores, the, 131
Condor Club, 23–24, 33, 38, 44–45
Cow Palace, the, 22–23, 40, 41
Creedence Clearwater Revival, 87, 137

Dakss, Jon, 94, 138
"Dance to the Medley" (song), 59, 185
Dance to the Music (album), 54, 56, 59, 60, 63, 80, 185
"Dance to the Music" (song), 58, 74, 84, 102, 154, 166, 185, 187
Davis, Betty, 102
Davis, Clive, 52, 90, 94, 122, 147, 170, 178
Davis, Jamie, 143, 147, 161
Davis, Martha, 135
Davis, Miles, 72, 92–93, 102–4, 114, 143
Day, Doris, 91, 115–116
DeMarino, Al, 51, 54, 60, 66–67, 79, 90, 97
Denton, Texas, 1–4, 124, 202
Dick Cavett Show, The, 83–84, 128
Dick Stewart Dance Party, 9, 21
Different Strokes by Different Folks (album), 147, 152, 184
Doda, Carol, 23–24, 33, 44, 80

Donahue, Tom ("Big Daddy"), 21, 22, 24, 27, 28, 40, 107–8, 123–124
"Don't Call Me Nigger, Whitey" (song), 69, 86, 168, 187
Dylan, Bob, 31, 87, 149
"Dynamite!" (song), 63, 64

Electric Circus, the, 51
Ellington, Duke, 18, 149
Epic Records, 19, 46–47, 52, 63, 90, 97, 105, 120, 123, 129, 152, 170
Errico, Greg, 35–36, 38–39, 48, 50, 53, 57, 59, 65, 68, 73, 92, 93, 102, 113, 139, 140, 141, 143, 145–147, 151–152, 159, 161, 172–173, 202
Errico, Jo, 36, 202
Errico, Mario, 36, 141–142, 159–160, 162, 165, 168, 169, 171, 202
Evangelist Temple Fellowship Center, 139, 155, 156–158, 160
"Everybody Is a Star" (song), 85, 167
"Everyday People" (song), 67–68, 84–85, 86, 142, 155

"Family Affair" (song), 91–92, 94, 96, 102, 114, 124, 188
Fillmore, the, 37, 44, 66–67, 183
Flamingo, the, 169
Flye, Tom, 108–111, 116–117, 119, 120–121
Fong-Torres, Ben, 28–29, 31, 72, 203
Franklin, Aretha, 44–45, 112
Freddie and the Stone Souls, 36–37, 38–39